WITHIN A YARD OF HELL

WITHIN A YARD
OF HELL

by

PHYLLIS THOMPSON

With a Foreword by MICHAEL TURNBULL

MOWBRAYS
LONDON & OXFORD

Copyright © 1963 by Phyllis Thompson

First published in 1963 by
Hodder & Stoughton

This edition published in 1979 by A. R.
Mowbray & Co., Ltd. Saint Thomas
House, Becket Street, Oxford OX1 1SJ

ISBN 0 264 66547 3

Printed in Great Britain by
Fletcher & Son Ltd, Norwich

Her own life transformed by reading
God in the Slums, Doreen Gemmel went
to Marble Arch, drawn by the need of
London's reckless women, to open "a
rescue shop within a yard of hell".

Some wish to live within the sound
Of church or chapel bell.
I want to run a rescue shop
Within a yard of hell.
                              C. T. Studd

Foreword

As I paused at some traffic lights on the outskirts of Nottingham, I hurriedly wound down the car window and hailed a man dressed in working clothes. 'Do you know the way to the Hospital for Women?' With the kind of efficiency unusual for such encounters he expertly gave the directions. As the lights turned to green and I was edging away, he glanced at my Church Army uniform and volleyed a parting shot, 'I hope you find Sister Gemmel in good heart!'

A chance in a thousand maybe but also a measure of Sister Gemmel's wide friendships and local fame. We had first been introduced some years earlier by another close friend of hers, Donald Coggan, then Archbishhop of York. In Nottingham she had undergone a series of major operations and as I entered the ward, I mentally prepared some suitable pastoral patter. It proved to be quite inappropriate as any concern for her health was brushed aside in a welter of questions about me, of rejoicings about nurses she was teaching to pray, and of praises for God who surrounded her bedside with his presence.

My next encounter with Sister Gemmel was at St Christopher's Hospice in South London where, though technically a resident, she was continuing an active ministry of counsellor and evangelist. I remember that after a brief exchange of news she said, 'Well, let's have some prayer together and then you must go as I have a busy afternoon.'

Such is the impact of this extraordinary woman of God. She has the true ability of a saint to give piercing concentration to the person with her and to offer insights of disturbing clarity. The visitor leaves with the distinct impression that his soul has been stripped and measured up for a completely new set of clothes.

7

Small wonder that countless people have to thank God for the ministry of Doreen Gemmel which has led them on the way of salvation. The theologian may ask what is it that we are saved from. To Doreen Gemmel's converts it is perfectly obvious for they have been introduced to the truth about themselves and then to the truth of God. To most of them the physical and social changes which result from conversion are apparent to all. Wilson Carlile, founder of the Church Army used to say, 'Go for the most lost'. It is a motto which Sister Gemmel has taken to heart and put into practice.

Each generation of Church Army Officers produces a handful of people who have the ability and courage to tackle some social problem in a unique and imaginative way. It is always risky and dangerous. It seems, to the establishment, doomed to failure. Above all, perhaps, it is costly in terms of the commitment and often the health of those involved. But that is of the essence of true evangelism. Programmes and · schemes and campaigns which cost nothing in terms of human beings are little more than pathetic shouts of ecclesiastical triumphalism. Doreen Gemmel is one of the best known Church Army evangelists in the tradition of sacrificial evangelism.

There are those who would seek to drive a wedge between a social gospel and a spiritual one. Some would seek to put bodies right before you tackle the soul. Others assume that social order will be the result of man turning to God. In the ministry of Doreen Gemmel there is no such division. Living conditions, family environment, personal fulfilment and the walk with God are all of a piece in the restoration of human beings to the image of their Maker.

That is why the story of Sister Gemmel has such an authentic ring and why there is a demand for this new edition of her life story. Here are no easy testimonies, but transparently true tales of people rescued and changed because of the singlemindedness of one woman. Given her vision no obstacle was too great, no person too important or powerful to stand in her way. As we read her story we cannot avoid asking questions about the integrity of our own ministry. But even more important than that, it gives us the hope and the vision that under God the impossible can happen, and that given faithful disciples he is able to achieve things beyond our wildest dreams.

MICHAEL TURNBULL

Chapter One

DOREEN GEMMEL had passed the barrier of the Glasgow railway terminus, and was walking rather aimlessly away from the platform when she caught sight of the bookstall. Under the domed glass roof, smoke-dimmed though it was, the books and periodicals on display showed up brightly enough, and glancing over them her eyes stopped at one, and a quick flicker of interest stirred in her mind. *God in the Slums.* That was the book she had heard someone speaking about recently. She could not remember what had been said about it, but the title had remained in her mind, and seeing it before her now she recognized it immediately. She had nothing in particular to do, so she decided to buy it.

"I'll go to MacDonald's for tea, and start reading it," she thought. The little book with its rather garish cover cost one shilling. She handed the money over to the man behind the counter, and walked off with the book under her arm, down the wide station approach to Argyle Street, where the trams rattled over the cobbles, and a few horse-drawn drays jostled with the ever-increasing motor traffic. She had not the slightest knowledge, as she crossed the busy road and walked along to the large high-class shop where she planned to have tea, that that little shilling book was to change the whole course of her life. Without expectation of anything unusual about to happen she made her way up to the third floor, into the large, low-ceilinged restaurant where well-to-do wives of Clydebank relaxed over tea and scones during their shopping expeditions, sat down at one of the square, white-clothed tables, and drew off her gloves. She looked around her indifferently, gave her order to the waitress, and opened the book.

It was written by a man who was seeking something to satisfy an inexplicable desire for a nobler life than that which he was living. Doreen's attention was arrested immediately, for deep calls to deep, and as she read on she became conscious of a corresponding desire in her own heart. She was gripped by the self-revealing manner in which the writer told the story, and did not pause in her reading until she came to the words:

"In those moments he came, unaware, to the brink of a spiritual precipice. So nearly did he miss it all; so nearly hesitating, too, have some of us come to grasping the enabling Hand which, just for a golden moment, has been stretched out to us in pity for 'the dullness of our blinded sight'."

She stopped at that sentence. Unaware she, too, had come to the brink of a spiritual precipice. She was thirty-two years of age, and although her life was secure enough materially, it did not satisfy her and she knew it. The round of theatre-going and dancing, the social whirl of parties in addition to constant activity as secretary to an eminent gynaecologist had filled her days and her evenings as well, but it had failed to provide her with a purpose for living. Indeed, it had all ended in a nervous breakdown, and that was why she was here in Scotland staying with her aunt rather than living in Liverpool with her mother. Aunt Peg always attended church, and surprisingly Doreen, who had never even gone to Sunday School when she was a little girl, felt happier with her than in her own home with its constant pleasure-seeking. Doreen could not really fathom Aunt Peg's evident contentment, but it had the effect of creating in her a conscious hunger for whatever it was that Aunt Peg possessed. And now, sitting in the restaurant with the book propped up before her, she knew that the golden moment had come and a Hand was stretched out—to her.

It was strange, perhaps, that the golden moment had not come to her sooner. Although her father, a well-to-do and popular doctor, had put his foot down against church-going himself, having had too much of it forced on him in his young days, he said, the Welsh nannie who reigned in the nursery did not fail to tell her little charge the 'stories of Jesus'. And if Doreen's beautiful mother was caught up in a whirl of social activity and gaiety, visits to Aunt Peg brought the little girl a knowledge of a different and more satisfying way of life. The years had not passed without opportunity for the tall, attractive, fair-haired girl to discover for herself that Spring of Life. But although there had often been a wistful longing for something, she knew not quite what, the delights and emotions of the moment had carried her along, skimming past the very waters for which her soul thirsted. Vital, emotional, the doctor's daughter had entered with enthusiasm into the gaiety of her parents' life; had experienced the dramatic tension of serving in canteens and driving Red Cross ambulances as a girl in her teens during World War I; had 'come out' officially at a ball, radiant in a shimmering evening dress; plunged into social life, dances, visits to theatres and race-courses; had taken up amateur dramatics with considerable success; became secretary to a specialist; had entered with all the ardour of her emotional nature into the sorrows of family bereavements; had accepted life as it presented itself to her, and had lived it to the full. But now, in the tea-room of the bustling Glasgow store, oblivious of the tinkle of teacups, the chatter of the shoppers, the hurrying back and forth of the waitresses, she realized as she read on through the pages of the shilling book that she had missed something. She was confronted with life of an entirely different character as she looked through the eyes of the Night Editor of a London daily at Salvation Army officers living in the slums. Here were young women like herself who were living in the midst of poverty and squalor, not by circumstances but by choice, cheerfully caring for old, sick people, cleaning filthy rooms, stretching out a helping hand wherever it was needed, often rewarded only with grumbling and ingratitude, but sometimes seeing lives transformed by the One of Whom they spoke. Hugh Redwood, the Night Editor, had seen something in their lives which never ceased to challenge him, and now she was seeing it, too.

She remembered her only personal contact with anyone in Salvation Army uniform. A year or two previously a young S.A. officer had called at the home of her employer with an envelope for Self-Denial Week. She had invited him into her office for a chat, and during the course of their conversation he had told her of a time when he and his wife were down to their last penny, and had prayed that God, who saw their need, would send them some money. Shortly afterwards the gas man had called to empty the meter, and counting over the coins it contained found a number left over, which he returned to them. "God answers prayer—He never fails," had been the confident assertion of the young S.A. officer. The few shillings which had meant so much to him seemed a paltry sum to the smart young secretary—but she realized dimly that he had something which she lacked. The incident had made its impression on her, and helped to quicken further her interest in what she was reading.

Something had happened more recently, too, which had stirred within her a consciousness of a better life than any she had known. Her uncle and Aunt Peg had taken her to stay at an hotel in Newtonmore in the Highlands, and while there a gentle, elderly man had talked to her about a place to which he often went when in London—the Church Army headquarters near Marble Arch, where a work was going on of reclaiming men and women from lives of sin and sorrow, with a remarkable man called Prebendary Carlile as leader. "That's the place for you!" old Mr. Jamieson had said, surprisingly. He had evidently sensed her restlessness and lack of vocation, and as he talked to her of life poured out in service for others, her attention had been gripped. The following Sunday, with her aunt in the little Scottish kirk, she had looked out through the open doors to see the sun going down in a blaze of glory behind the purple hills, and listened, awed yet stimulated by the words that were being sung,

> Take up thy Cross, the Saviour said,
> If thou wouldst My disciple be;
> Deny thyself, the world forsake,
> And humbly follow after Me.

The words seemed directly for her, searching her with their challenge and the uncompromising nature of their call. But she did not know how to respond, what to do. It was as though a glimpse had been granted her of a Man whose face was set steadfastly to go to a Cross, and who called her to follow. But the vision faded. She did not know how to recapture it, and had returned to the aimless life of reading, resting, driving around in the car, trying to regain the old vitality and to overcome the nameless fear that had haunted her ever since the night some months ago, when she had suddenly collapsed at home, and had been ordered a complete rest. She had walked in darkness all these months, but now, suddenly, sitting in the Glasgow restaurant with the book propped up before her, she knew that the golden moment had come for her. She was brought to a standstill at last, the emotions, the fears, the excitements that had agitated her mind subdued by a Presence she only dimly apprehended, but which she nevertheless recognized. Like the blind man who, centuries before, sat by Jericho's highwayside, she realized that "Jesus of Nazareth passeth by". His was the enabling hand that was stretched out now.

How long she sat there silent, looking at those words, she did not know. Eventually she put the book in her bag, paid her bill and walked out of the restaurant. As one in a dream she wandered around the shops, made a few purchases, and then retraced her steps up the slope into St. Enoch's station, and started on the journey back to her aunt's home. Usually it was a relief to get out of the great sprawling city with its tightly-packed rows of tall tenement houses, its grey, cobbled streets and smoke-grimed factories, and emerge into the open country. But today Doreen was too deeply engrossed in her book even to notice the fleeting shadows of clouds drifting across the soft, green hills that roll down to the Clyde estuary. When she reached grey-roofed little Kilmacolm nestling among the trees, and made her way along the uphill road that led out of the town, her thoughts were far away, groping as it were for something she had glimpsed again as she read of the sorrows and sin, the humour and humanity found in London's slums. And by the time she came to the solid, square-faced house right on the edge of the moor, and mounted the steep way up to the front door it was as though strong tendrils were reaching towards her from the alleys and back streets of the city, twining themselves round her heart, drawing her to those places where there were unknown people—in need.

The need. That was what was drawing her, though she could not have defined it. Away there in that world of squalor and poverty there were men and women and little children in need,

14

and it was a need deeper than she could fathom. It drew her with a strange magnetic power, and it called to something within her that she had not realized was there—a capacity for sacrifice. It was quite inexpressible, that sense of the awakening of yearning to spend and be spent in the service of the dwellers in the slums. And beyond that desire she was deeply conscious of a deeper yearning still—a yearning to follow the One whose call to forsake the world she had heard in the little highland kirk. Could it be that He was to be found, after all, not amid the beauty of the hills and dales under the open heavens, but in the sordid back streets of the cities?

Doreen said little about her feelings when she reached home, although she showed the book to her aunt, and commented on it. But her mind was still preoccupied as she sat at the dinner table that night, and the snowy linen and sparkling glass accorded ill with her thoughts. She was thinking of the poverty and degradation amongst which those cheerful Salvation Army officers were living, and as the evening progressed, and she relaxed in the understanding sympathy of her aunt, she found herself talking of what she had read in that book, and suddenly she gave expression to the thought that had been crystallizing in her mind, as she fired the question: "What would happen if I went to work in the slums?"

She could not have given voice to such a fantastic suggestion to anyone but Aunt Peg. Worldly, knowing nothing of the seamy side of life, only slowly recovering from a nervous breakdown, who was she to embark on such a service? It would have been reasonable if Aunt Peg, delighted though she was at this sudden return of Doreen's old vitality, had answered with caution, advising her to wait for full recovery of health before engaging on anything so likely to upset the nerves as slum visitation.

Human reason, however, was not at the helm on this day of the golden moment. A greater and wiser power was in control, and Aunt Peg responded to it without any resistance. Looking across at the flushed face of the niece she loved as a daughter, she answered the question simply and quietly in words that Doreen never forgot.

"If it is God's will," she said, "you must go."

Chapter Two

THE SLUMS. Doreen knew nothing whatever about them beyond what she had seen from railway trains as they drew in and out of the great termini of Glasgow or Liverpool or London. Looking out of the windows of railway compartments she had glanced with distaste at the rows and rows of squalid streets and into the little backyards where dustbins and dilapidated prams, brooms and pans and broken boxes were jumbled together. If the thought had ever crossed her mind that human beings were living out their lives within the walls of the dingy houses with their curtainless windows like glassy, soulless eyes, it had made no impression on her consciousness. There was rarely any sign of life to be seen from the train, only the stony desert of asphalt and brick and mortar where the grimy green of an occasional stunted tree bore silent evidence to the fact that underneath it all, buried but not dead, lay warm Mother Earth. And as the train gathered speed along the track that led to fairer scenes, or drew in under the roof of the terminus, the memory of those forbidding silent walls and narrow streets faded before it registered. The slums had concealed their secrets. The closest glimpse she had gained of them was through the eyes of the Night Editor who had seen God at work in them, and it was that glimpse which had stirred in her the desire to see likewise.

It was significant that the stirring of that desire seemed to improve her health. As she awoke each morning now, it was with a sense of having a purpose in life, and she quite forgot that she was recovering from a breakdown. She was no longer conscious of weariness, nor did she feel light-headed. In fact, she did not feel anything, so absorbed was she with the thought of the slums, and with wondering by what means she could get to them.

If her aunt observed the sudden change in her erstwhile languid niece she wisely refrained from more than a passing comment, and when Doreen announced that she intended writing to the Salvation Army, did nothing to deter her. So it came about that a letter was dispatched to the Salvation Army headquarters from Doreen Burns-Gemmel, indicating that she was concerned about the needs of the people in the slums, and offering her services if there was anything she could do amongst them. She did not explain what she thought she could do, but expected it would be a ladylike little task of afternoon visiting two or three times a a week, and pictured herself sallying forth with a basket of groceries on her arm to dispense the necessities of life to starving families or lonely old-age pensioners. A sort of visitor for the Salvation Army, she thought; and expected that her offer would be accepted without question. She was therefore quite unprepared for the reply which she received. It came in a very large envelope, and apart from a courteous but brief covering letter, consisted of a highly decorative document entitled:

THE SALVATION ARMY

ARTICLES OF WAR

at the bottom of which was a red seal with the words 'Blood and Fire'. This document, it was pointed out, was required to be signed by all wishing to be enrolled as soldiers of the Salvation Army.

Doreen examined it with surprise and consternation. The picture of an old man with a long white beard called 'The Founder' adorned one corner, while opposite him was a sweet-faced woman in a bonnet who was 'The Army Mother'. Below her were little pictures with texts under them—a man preaching, a mother teaching her children, and a Salvation Army officer motioning a tramp to enter an open door.

As Doreen read the words, "Bring the poor that are cast out into thy house" underneath that last picture, was there any quickening response in her mind? Was there, just for a moment, a lifting of the veil that hides the future? Did she, even then, hear for the first time, as from a long distance, the cry of the outcast?

Perhaps not. Perhaps it is only in retrospect that the aptness of that little sentence of commission can be seen like a directing finger pointing the way she must go. She turned her attention to the declaration that she would be required to sign if she were to be enrolled as a soldier of the Salvation Army, and found that she could not make head or tail of it. It referred to receiving salvation, being wholly sanctified, and renouncing the world with all its sinful pleasures. It spoke of conversion, of the power of the Spirit of God to take away evil tendencies, of the eternal happiness of the righteous and the endless punishment of the wicked. She saw that if she signed it she would be vowing, not only to abstain from intoxicating liquors, bad language, the reading of obscene books and falsehood in any shape or form, but also that "believing solemnly that The Salvation Army has been raised up by God and is sustained and directed by Him" to carry out to the utmost of her ability all its orders and regulations.

Regretfully Doreen sent back the Articles of War unsigned. She was very sorry, she wrote, but she really knew nothing about the Salvation Army except the uniform. And that, she thought, closed the matter. But there she was wrong. A few days later she received another letter on Salvation Army stationery, asking if she would like to go to live for a time in a slum post in Edinburgh as a Sergeant. There was no mention of signing anything, but it was suggested that if the idea appealed to her she could meet the Slum Post Officer from Edinburgh to discuss the matter. It did not occur to her until long afterwards that it would also be the task of the Slum Post Officer to 'size her up'.

Doreen wrote by return, warmly accepting the offer. To go and actually live in the slums with Salvation Army 'lasses' was better than anything she had expected. "Does this mean she's going to stagger about in uniform, banging drums at street corners?" wrote her brother, half-horrified, half-amused at the manner in which his emotional younger sister was recovering from her breakdown. Other members of the family discussed the matter with varying degrees of dismay, and her mother travelled up from Liverpool to Glasgow to see for herself the condition of her daughter who had suddenly become 'religious'. Certainly

Doreen looked better, and behaved quite rationally, the mother observed, but she was different. There was a new quality in her smile, her manner, and above all in her purpose. She was no longer rather excitably on the alert for some new experience, or planning some pleasure as before her illness, neither had she the somewhat bewildered, almost frightened look in her eyes that had come into them since the day when she had so suddenly and alarmingly collapsed. Her eyes were calm enough, and surprisingly happy in one who was about leave the comfort that amounted to luxury for the squalor of the slums. It was this entirely new direction in which her daughter was travelling that dismayed Mrs. Burns-Gemmel. The child whom she had thought she knew so well had suddenly developed qualities which made her almost a stranger, and as she sat in the train on her return journey to Liverpool on the day before Doreen was to leave for Edinburgh and the slums, it was with a strange sense of bereavement. She felt that she had 'lost' her daughter. And in a sense, she had. The ways had parted because the hearts had parted, and the social life which satisfied the mother no longer held any attraction for the daughter. Can two walk together unless they be agreed? Years later when Mrs. Gemmel herself began to walk the path of Life there was unity and understanding between them such as they had never known before together, but at this stage the whole thing was incomprehensible to the older woman.

Meanwhile Doreen herself was preparing with enthusiasm for the new life. Not least of its attractions was the fact that she would be in uniform again. Something in her responded with deep approval to the regimental loyalty demanded by the wearing of a uniform, and she had stood to attention, eyes front, with the best of them as a Girl Guide Commissioner or a member of the V.A.D. during the First World War. The discipline which some natures rebelled against she found infinitely satisfying, and had no difficulty in accepting the control imposed by the ringing of bells and blowing of whistles.

It was a red-letter day, and one for ever blazoned on her memory when, on February 19, 1931, she donned a red Salvation Army jersey, her navy blue Guide commissioner uniform, and a navy blue hat, and set off on the journey from Glasgow to Edinburgh resembling as much as possible a member of the Salvation Army without actually being one. She was 'in a command' again, and this time a command connected, not with an earthly kingdom, but a heavenly. There was a note of exultation in her heart, too, in the realization that there was a call to sacrifice in this command. As with many another, the warning of 'sweat and blood and toil and tears' drew her into battle rather than deterred her from it, and the prospect of a life involving hardship and privation was strangely attractive.

Compared with the background from which she had come, hardship and privation was certainly what she entered into now. Many a time, in the past, she had looked across the Princes Garden ravine that divides Edinburgh socially as well as geographically, admiring the city's distinctive skyline. Beautiful it always seemed to her, from the famous old castle, along the turrets and sharp pointed steeples of the Royal Mile that plunged down to Holyrood Palace, and on to the steep humped hill of Arthur's Seat and the long cliff line of Salisbury Crag. As a Scot Doreen had often gazed with pride at that skyline, and a lump had come into her throat as she recalled the courage and loyalty of the men who had defended it. But as for what was happening under it now, what were the unrecorded human histories being lived out in the tenements and the narrow alleys, the attics and the cellars in the area 'behind the castle', she knew nothing at all about them. The people who strolled along Princes Street in those days, before its exclusiveness was invaded by Woolworths and Marks and Spencer were those who lived in social security 'before the castle', and only when they swept along to functions at the Castle or Holyrood Palace were they likely to leave their side of Princes Gardens. But now Doreen found herself riding in a tramcar past the familiar entrance of the Caledonian Hotel, escorted by a little Salvation Army lieutenant with curly hair, merry eyes and a pronounced Irish accent who led her across the road and up the slope under the shadow of the Castle to the top of the Royal Mile.

"Here we are," she said as they came to a long, curved terrace of lock-up shops and public houses over which rose storey after storey of windows, some shabbily curtained, some blank and empty with broken panes. She opened a street door next to a public house and went in, Doreen following her into what seemed complete darkness until, stumbling forward, she saw she was at the bottom of a stone spiral stairway lighted dimly by a skylight four storeys above. She started to count the steps as they mounted to the first storey where there were four front doors, uncompromisingly shut, then to the second with another four doors, and then up to the third. "Seventy-six," muttered Doreen as her guide said reassuringly, "Home at last," and producing a key opened the door to the quaintest little habitation Doreen had ever entered. A narrow passage faced her, half-way along which a door opened to reveal a small cupboard in which, to her amazement, she saw what appeared to be half a bath built into the wall. "That's the bath-tub room," she was informed. "We have a bath there once a week—heat the water on the kitchen stove . . . Here's the kitchen. We've put a bed up for you here. No spare room, I'm afraid."

The kitchen was small, and what with the sink in the corner by the window, a small table and a couple of chairs, the bucket of coal by the black kitchen range, and the iron bedstead that was pushed up against the wall, there was little enough room for Doreen's suitcases. "The bedroom's through there," she was told. "But come ye right along and have tea—it's in the front room. We've got a fish custard today."

Doreen little realized as she sat down at the front room table with its simple white cloth and coarse but pretty crockery what thought and care had gone into the preparation of this meal. Accustomed as she was to a four-course dinner, with a well-trained parlour-maid standing behind her right shoulder to pour wine and unobtrusively remove her plate, it was a new experience to eat fish custard with tea, followed by bread and margarine and jam, the dirty plates being stacked in a pile on the corner of the table. Only after she had been in the Slum Post for several days did she learn what a rare delicacy was fish custard—fish *and* egg *and* milk, all at one meal! But the Adjutant who had turned up (in mufti) for the first meeting with Doreen in Glasgow, wanted to make her entry into a Slum Post as easy as possible. And what could be more appetizing than fish custard at high tea, before going off to the evening meeting in 'the hall' down the Royal Mile? So they sat together for tea, the little Irish girl who but a few years later was to lay down her life among typhoid victims in the Congo; Doreen; and the short, stocky Scotswoman who was in charge of the Slum Post, 'the Adjutant' in whose home Doreen still said, a quarter of a century later, that she first saw 'the footprints of the Divine.'

Chapter Three

IN THE nine weeks that followed it was the personality of 'my Adjutant' that unconsciously dominated all the impressions made upon the young woman launched so suddenly on a way of life entirely new to her. Intensely human was the Adjutant, with a rare sense of humour, a brisk businesslike way of doing things, and an insatiable interest in her fellow creatures which drew her, an eager spectator, to any stir in the street. Only the sternest and most pressing duty could carry her past a church door if a bride were about to appear! When 'Leff' as the Lieutenant was affectionately called, returned from an afternoon spent collecting old clothes from the back doors of the well-to-do for a jumble sale, Adjutant dived into the sack with the utmost enthusiasm to see what it contained. "What, *another* pair of O.D.s!" she would exclaim as she held up for inspection an article of clothing that always seemed to be in good supply. "Och, do they think we wear nothing else, here behind the castle?"

But through the cheerful, hearty personality of her new commander Doreen saw something else which both awed and drew her, for to the Adjutant God was a reality and Jesus was a friend. Her worship of God was with those 'deepest, tenderest fears' which made her scrupulously honest and conscientious in her personal life, and fortified her to face cruelty and sin with eyes blazing with an indignation before which brutal men shrank ashamed. The Adjutant would walk fearlessly into scenes and situations which would have caused the pluckiest policeman to hesitate, and surprisingly no one ever seemed to question her right to do so. But the eyes that blazed with anger were softened with compassion as she looked on suffering and sorrow, and she was ready at any hour of the day or night to respond to a call for help.

"Adjutant, that puir auld Mrs. McPherson is wheezing that pitiful . . . could ye come?"

"Adjutant, those chillen in the room opposite hasn't had a bite these two days . . ."

"Tell the Adjutant to come quick! The man upstairs is a-dyin' . . ."

Immediately the sturdy little woman would be on her feet. "I'm coming," she would say. "Leff, if I'm not back in time you see about pricing the jumble . . . and don't wait dinner . . ." And down the seventy-six steps she would go off to some dingy room to bring the relief that her very presence, with its resourcefulness and calm assurance seemed to convey to those in need. Sometimes Doreen was taken along, and later sent to clean windows, wash clothes, carry buckets of coal for sufferers in the slums. She became accustomed to the streets of terraced houses where front doors opened out on to the pavement, where torn wallpaper hung limply from moist walls in rooms with dirty, unmade beds, and damp washing dangled from lines across the ceiling. Her nose learned to detect when a building was afflicted with bed bugs or bad drains or both, as she made her way along dark passages where dirty children, noses running, played with mangy cats. Those were the days of the trade depression when queues of men lined up daily at the labour exchanges, and their women at home starved themselves to feed the children. For those women the jumble sales were their only hope of obtaining clothing for the family, and the Adjutant knew it. The need for plenty of jumble, therefore, was ever before her, and she did not hesitate to mention it in her prayers.

To Doreen, accustomed only to prayers said in churches, the inclusion of such subjects, along with pleas for the conversion of sinners and deliverance for sufferers, all spoken extempore, in broad Scotch, kneeling on the shabby lino of the kitchen floor, brought a deep sense of the presence of the unseen Friend on whom Adjutant unquestionably relied. She knelt by her hard chair, head bowed on her hands, awed, subdued, yet satisfied in a way she had never known was possible. This, then, was what she had so nearly missed when, all unknown, she had come to the brink of the spiritual precipice. This was what the enabling Hand, stretched out to her in that golden moment, was drawing her to.

The shabby little room faded, and she was conscious only of a stillness that throbbed with life, and which enveloped her very soul in a deeper content than she had ever known. It seemed that were she to open her eyes she would see Him standing there, the Man of Galilee, so conscious was she of His presence. So she bowed her head low, in exquisite awe and devotion, until eventually, quieted and strengthened, she rose to her feet with the others as they turned again to the duties of the day.

"How wonderful it is to walk with God," she hummed cheerfully as she set about the tasks allotted to her. It was the first line of a hymn she learned in the Slum Post and she smiled to herself often as she saw what that walk involved. It was all so different from anything she had previously associated with the 'religious life', in which no thought of domestic duties had ever entered. Here in the Slum Post it was up before 7 a.m. to black-lead the kitchen range ('Leff' took pity on the perplexed Doreen, and showed her how to do it), and down the seventy-six steps after 10 p.m. to shake the mats out of the front door, with the hours between filled with shopping, cleaning, cooking, calling at front doors to collect 'Self-Denial' envelopes and at back doors to beg for jumble; visiting the sick to put their rooms in order; leading meetings in the 'Hall', a room on the first floor of a tenement house down the Royal Mile, opposite John Knox' House—and conducting jumble sales there, too. On one occasion Doreen was startled to see Adjutant hold up for auction an article of clothing which she recognized as her own, and from the back of the hall she went hurrying to the front calling aloud, amid shouts and laughter, "Adjutant, that's *my laundry*!"

Here too, she preached her first sermon, commanded to do so by Adjutant who waved aside her protestations that she had never preached in her life. "Och!" she said. "We've all got to start. You can do it all right. You ask the Lord to give you the message and help you to tell it out, and He will. We've all got to speak for Jesus in the Army!" So Doreen wrote to Aunt Peg asking her to send all the books she could think of that might help her to speak at the Gospel meeting, and painstakingly prepared a talk on the resurrection, choosing as her text, "After

25

that He was seen of about 500 brethren at once; of whom the greater part remain unto this present . . ." She wrote it out word for word, carrying the paper with her wherever she went, and learned it off by heart, repeating it on tramcars, as she walked along the street, even standing at doors waiting for them to open after her knock. The thought of delivering this address weighed heavily on her mind, and she was cold with tension on the appointed evening as she walked up the dirty stone stairs leading to the 'Hall'. She looked apprehensively at the rows of heavy, wooden benches, the bare floor, and the platform on which she must stand alone in the unsoftened light before the shabbily clad men with caps pulled low over their foreheads, and the weary, untidy women who would be there to listen to her. But Adjutant smiled at her encouragingly. "You'll be all right. I'll be praying for you, and the Lord'll help you." When at last the moment came to rise to her feet amid the hush that followed the closing of hymn-books and the shuffling into position on the benches, she gave out her text and forgot her nervousness altogether. And after it was finished, and the last hymn, with its appeal to "Come, come, come," was being sung, what was her joy to see a woman, head low, come walking nervously up the aisle, and drop on her knees at the penitent form. "God was with you, Sergeant . . . ! the first time you speak you win a soul for Jesus!" Adjutant said later, her eyes glowing. "God was with you!"

For Doreen, however, the most outstanding evidence that God was with her was not when things went well, but on a day when things went ill, and she found herself facing tirades of abuse at front doors. She had been sent to collect the little envelopes marked 'Self-Denial' which had been slipped into the letter boxes in a certain street some days previously. She was told to knock at each front door, and when it was opened to say pleasantly that she had called to collect the Self-Denial envelope. In some cases, she was assured, it would be handed to her with something in it, and in some cases it probably would not, and she gathered that she must do as occasion served whatever response she received to her knock. Little realizing what awaited her she set out, dressed in her navy blue Guide Commissioner uniform, with the red jersey and headgear unique to the Salvation Army. The street to which she was sent was in a typical working-class area, and by the time she had knocked at a dozen front doors she was feeling bewildered and battered. Why was it that as soon as some of those doors opened, before she had spoken so much as a word, a torrent of scorn and indignation against the Salvation Army in general, and herself as its tangible representative in particular, poured out to her? She knew nothing about a controversy connected with the organization which was receiving publicity in the press at that time, and in which some sections of the public were expressing strong opinions based on very inadequate information. She had no idea what the people who stood at their front doors, shouting at her, were talking about, and she really did not care, either, for as she proceeded along the street it dawned on her that something had happened to her. These people who were her social inferiors, speaking insultingly to her, evoked no irritation, much less anger, in her heart. She was amazed at herself. That she, Doreen Burns-Gemmel, only daughter of Dr. Burns-Gemmel of Liverpool, should be knocking at front doors in a slum area politely asking for Self-Denial envelopes was beyond the bounds of anything she would have imagined possible three months ago. That she should mildly stand and be shouted at was almost incredible. How her eye would have flashed, and her tongue stung with quietly spoken, cutting scorn if this had happened before reading *God in the Slums*! But now she had no feeling of contempt, no reaction of anger, only of wonder that she was so changed. There was but one explanation for it. "God must have done it for me," she thought. "I can't understand it—it's marvellous! Whatever it is they're so enraged about I don't know, and it's certainly not my fault. I can't think why I'm not furious at them speaking to me like this, but I'm not. This must be that I'm converted—that it's happened to *me*!"

So the weeks sped by in this new life in which laughter and humour flashed constantly against the background of poverty and hardship in which the Salvation Army workers spent their days. There was the time when the woman who delivered the bread carefully wrapped around with a piece of strong brown

27

paper arrived one day greatly distressed that the precious brown paper was missing. "I dunno what's happened to it," she said, and continued, unaware of the effect her words were having on her hearers, "I uses it to bring your bread of a morning, and then I uses it to wrap up me husband's wooden leg when he takes it off at night, and now I've lost it . . ." And the occasion when, late one night, the mousetrap under the sink went off and Doreen, horrified, hastily emptied its contents out of the front window. The dead mouse unfortunately landed into the hat of a passer-by, whose reaction was prompt and lucid, and quite unmixed with grace. And there was 'Leff's' never to be forgotten remark when entering the kitchen after bedtime she saw Doreen, whose habits of close attention to her personal appearance had not yet dropped off, her creamed hands in white cotton gloves, and bed socks on her feet for warmth. "Gracious, Sergeant!" exclaimed the astonished Irish girl. "All you need's goloshes and an umbrella!"

How long she would have remained in the Edinburgh Slum Post if her brother had not arrived on the scene is uncertain. As far as she was concerned she was prepared to stay there for life. She had never before been so happy, and although on her weekly half-day off she visited one of her aunts who lived 'before the castle', and there consumed quantities of cream and cakes with whole-hearted enjoyment, she always returned to the top of the Royal Mile with the feeling that she was coming home. She did not realize that the transition from a leisurely life in which well-cooked, heavy meals played a prominent part to days of ceaseless activity on a frugal diet was too sudden for her constitution, and that she was losing weight. When her brother came to Edinburgh for the Rugby International Match and saw her waiting to meet him on the station platform at 6 a.m., therefore, he was shocked at her appearance, and promptly wrote to their mother saying this was all nonsense and would have to stop, for 'Dody' was killing herself. There followed letters urging her to return to Kilmacolm and see the doctor, and such maternal pleas could not be ignored. The outcome was that the doctor said the work was too hard for her and she should give it up, although he did add that it would not be very suitable for her to return to doing nothing but the daily shopping!

Sadly she received the verdict and broke the news to the distressed Adjutant, who decided that at any rate the 'Sergeant' should have a good send-off from the Slum Post, and with a strangely heavy heart made arrangements for a farewell meeting in the 'Hall'. Not only Aunt Peg, but Doreen's mother came to this, and occupied a place on the platform. For Mrs. Burns-Gemmel the ordeal reached a climax when she found herself standing self-consciously at attention while everybody else sang a chorus:

> *A robe of white, a crown of gold,*
> *A hope, a harp, a mansion fair . . .*

enthusiastically accompanied by actions—hands drawn down the body for the robe of white, followed by the donning of an imaginary crown, the playing of an imaginary harp, and finally pointing upwards to the invisible mansions.

"Do the actions, mother!" hissed Doreen urgently, noting with dismay her mother's immobility. Aunt Peg was making a valiant effort to make the suitable gestures, and Doreen was conscious that her mother's was the only rigid figure on the platform. But Mrs. Burns-Gemmel could go no farther. She was devoted to her children, and would not have hesitated to die for them had circumstances demanded such a sacrifice. If her only daughter chose to don Salvation Army uniform and behave in a wholly incomprehensible way she would stand by her, just as she would if she had committed a felony and had to appear in court. That was why she was in this bare-looking hall tonight, standing in full view of the rows of shabbily-dressed people, some of whom she suspected had come in the worse for drink. But to start waving her arms about to the cheerful throb of a few brass instruments and a tambourine was more than she felt could be expected of her. The robe, the crown, the harp and the mansion failed to evoke any response from her, and she stood to attention in her smart cloche hat and elegant costume, rigid right to the end.

Chapter Four

THERE ARE ways in life which appear to lead into a backwater, but which prove to be the channel of the main stream, waters that look stagnant, but which are in reality being moved by an unseen current. When Doreen left Edinburgh to return to her aunt's comfortable home in Kilmacolm it seemed as though she were back where she had started before she responded to the powerful impulse to go and live in the slums. Her future course was as obscure as it had been before. But she returned to Kilmacolm a different woman, and knew she could never again settle into the old existence of outward ease with all its inward restlessness. Even before leaving the little flat at the top of the Royal Mile she was looking around for some other cause into which she could throw herself, and put out feelers in at least one direction. There was a worthy organization which produced women church workers, and wondering if this would prove to be her calling in life she pursued her enquiries to the extent of going for a personal interview. It proved wholly unsatisfactory from her point of view. The emphasis regarding the career about which she was enquiring was not on the work to be done or the needs to be met, but rather on the long holidays granted to those considered suitable. The year   appeared, was divided into terms as in schools, sand-wiched between delectable periods during which no demands would be made on the worker, who could go where she liked and do what she would. The prospect of such a life after the activity and tension and constant demands of the unexpected in the Slum Post, so far from attracting her, filled her with dismay, and the interview terminated with the mutual understanding that that was the end of it.

There followed a short pause in the course of events rather like the silence that follows the throb and clash of a stimulating over-ture. She was back in the familiar round of a well-organized, well-to-do household with no claims on her time. It had to be. It was in the quietness of that pause that her life was re-directed. Nothing startling happened, no dramatic revelation or vision was seen, no voice heard. But quite simply, almost imperceptibly, memory brought to the surface a conversation of some months previously. Her mind went back to the gentle old man in the hotel in the Highlands who had talked to her about something that was happening at Marble Arch—a work going on amongst 'down-and-outs'—an organization with a name that was somewhat militant, like the Salvation Army. Mentioning this to Aunt Peg she learned, to her surprise, that Aunt Peg not only knew the body she was talking about, but actually sent regular donations to it and received reports of its activities. It was called the Church Army, and had been founded by a man named Wilson Carlile some years after William Booth founded the Salvation Army. In many respects the two organizations were similar. Both were composed mainly of lay men and women with no outstanding educational attainments or social advantages, who were pre-pared to devote their lives to helping the poor and the outcasts of society. Wilson Carlile himself had been a highly successful young business man until the failure of the bank in which his money was invested brought him to the realization of the im-permanence of earthly foundations. Physically affected by the blow to his fortunes, it was while he was flat on his back that the reading of one chapter of a book* had faced him so convinc-ingly with the utter worthlessness of his life and the rottenness of what he had previously considered a decent, respectable character, that then and there, on the sofa, he had prayed to God for for-giveness and knew he had received it. This simple transaction of soul resulted in a complete change of aim and purpose. Within a few years the young business man had taken Holy Orders, and was enthusiastically conducting open air meetings in slum areas which drew such large crowds that on occasion traffic had to be diverted! When his Vicar reluctantly explained that this sort of thing would have to stop or the Church would be running foul of the police, Carlile turned his attention to another means of

* *Grace and Truth* by Mackay.

attaining the same end—that of proclaiming to as many people as possible that Jesus is alive today, and ready to forgive. As it was such a simple message, needing no qualifications to proclaim beyond a personal experience of its efficacy, why not encourage and train ordinary people to tell it to others? He already had a little band of working men who had been helping in his meetings, and finding that in two or three other London parishes clergymen had formed teams in a similar way, he suggested that they should be banded together as an adjunct to the Church of England. In 1882 the Church Army was formed. Starting with some hundred or more men, women were later enlisted and in the subsequent years these Captains and Sisters have developed a world-wide organization engaged in what we call to-day "*practical Christianity.*" Their evangelistic and social welfare work covers every sphere of life and their Homes and Hostels are famous throughout England. And the constant emphasis of Prebendary Wilson Carlile was still on reaching the people who were beyond the pale of respectable society—the drunkards, the fallen, the criminals. When a drunken man reeled into church one Sunday evening and was about to be escorted discreetly out by the sidesmen Carlile called from the pulpit, "Hi, don't let him go! I want him!" and then, to add emphasis, he waved his hand in a gesture to include everyone in the church and continued, "All the rest of you can go if you like—but keep him!" The constant butt of mocking loungers in the streets, who pelted him on occasion with cabbage stumps and rotten vegetables, he came up cheerful and smiling, and with his ready wit often won those who were his tormenters. "You've given me a good time out here," he said to one such youth who had managed to trip him over in the road, to the huge delight of the onlookers. "Now come inside, and I'll give *you* a good time!" Enjoying the unusual circumstances, the youth went in, calling the crowd in after him. The unexpected outcome was that that night his whole life was transformed, and to the astonishment of his companions he took his place in the religious processions that he had previously jeered at. Many were the stories of similar sorties led by the remarkable leader of the Church Army, and although Aunt Peg could tell her little enough, what she heard heightened Doreen's interest. Could it be that there was a place for her in the organization that had such a leader?

She decided to find out. She sat down and wrote a letter to the Church Army, enquiring if there were any openings for service in its ranks for a woman like herself, over thirty and with no training in church work. It did not seem very likely that there were, but she posted the letter all the same, and the reply came on a day when she and her aunt were in Edinburgh, staying 'before the castle' in the Caledonian Hotel on Princes Street. When she saw the envelope and realized where it came from she opened it immediately, standing in the lounge of the hotel, and read on the first page words which arrested her.

"This little booklet is dedicated to young women with a deep consecration of life and purpose who, at the call of Christ, offer themselves for His service."

Here was something to respond to! Work and sacrifice were expected of her if she joined the Church Army. Her approval was won at once. But there was something else. At the top of the same page she was almost startled to read the words:

"The Master is come, and calleth for thee."

There was an imperative ring about that little booklet, a stirring to action which the accompanying letter, couched in kind terms but holding out little hope to one of her age, could not deaden. Standing there in the luxury of one of Edinburgh's smartest hotels, as indelible an impression was made upon her as in the little kirk in the Scottish Highlands months before. But this time the vision was clearer, and she knew what to do. On returning to Kilmacolm she set herself to write another letter to the Church Army, and carefully thought out what she wanted to say. It was not without a sense of urgency that she scribbled on the back of the envelope in which the booklet had come some words which she felt best expressed what she meant: " . . . as it is to be my life

33

work I want to make very certain that I am choosing the path in which I can do most for the Master."

The letter was duly written and posted, but the sense of urgency increased as she waited for a reply, and with characteristic impulsiveness she acted.

Quite out of the blue I decided one day to go up to London alone. Up to now my only visits there had been to stay in an hotel with friends, and go shopping, sightseeing, to shows. I remember finding the address of a guest house in Regent's Park in the Guider's magazine, and suddenly one afternoon fixing to go by train from Glasgow the next day. That may sound very ordinary and an everyday happening now, but for me it was a very real adventure. My life had been a sheltered one in the way of always having my family and friends around me. The morning after my arrival in London I was very undecided as to to my next move, but finally made up my mind to telephone to the Church Army.

She found the number in the telephone book, put through her call and was invited to go along that same morning to be interviewed by Miss Carlile, sister of Wilson Carlile and leader of the women's work. So she set off for the neighbourhood that was to become so familiar to her that she knew every road and every little cobbled mews slipping furtively away behind the rows of tall, dignified houses and tree-lined squares. But on this memorable morning it was all new to her, and she followed the main streams of traffic running from Marylebone Road, along Baker Street and out into Marble Arch via Oxford Street. She was too absorbed in anticipating the probable course of the impending interview to give more than a cursory glance at the roads she was travelling as she proceeded towards her destination. At last she arrived at a rather narrow street and came to a standstill outside the porticoed entrance of a long, four-storeyed building, only separated from the pavement by iron railings and a narrow basement area. There was little to distinguish it from other buildings in the neighbourhood, and she paused a moment to

34

ensure that she had arrived at the right place. Then she rang the bell at a heavy, old-fashioned front door which opened on to a small, rather dark, uninspiring hall. But thirty years later Doreen, remembering it as clearly as if it had happened yesterday, wrote:

The moment I crossed the threshold I knew without a shadow of doubt that that was where God wanted me to be.

Chapter Five

SISTER HUMBY was at her wits' end. Neat as always, outwardly calm and efficient, she simply did not know what to do. There was the redoubtable Mrs. Simpson in the hall, eyes glaring fiercely, obviously very drunk, ringing for all she was worth the big brass bell used to summon the probationers to lectures. The distressed young probationer who had innocently opened the front door in response to her knock and been pushed unceremoniously aside when the tornado swept in stood by, helplessly, as the others came flocking down the stairs, up from the kitchen, out from the common-room, at the urgent note of that bell, to come to a dismayed standstill as they saw the stout form in the middle of the hall. They all knew Mrs. Simpson and had learned to give her a wide berth when she was in her cups. She was a familiar figure in the streets around the Marble Arch end of Edgware Road, and it was no idle boast of hers that she would tackle a couple of policemen at once if they tried to interfere with her. Sister Humby, Warden of the women's work of the Training College knew her well, and gave strict orders that she was not to be admitted into the College. But now that the bustling, powerful woman had forced her own way in, there was no hope of getting her out again without creating a noisy and undignified scene. Until such time as she elected to depart, there Mrs. Simpson must remain. And when would that be? The bell continued ringing furiously, the probationers clustered around, some giggling, some shocked, when Sister Humby suddenly had an inspiration.

"Leave her alone," she whispered to the student nearest to her. "Tell the girls to come and pray." And so the hall emptied, leaving only that furious figure brandishing the bell, while the young women went down on their knees and prayed that God would make Mrs. Simpson stop ringing the bell and go quietly home. They did not omit to request that He would eventually save her soul, but for the present distress the most urgent prayer was that she might quieten down and depart. And as they prayed, the bell did stop ringing, and a blessed silence fell in the hall outside. Prayer had been answered! With varying expressions of wonder and unbelief they arose and tiptoed out, only to see the object of their concern, tired of bell ringing, sitting on the stairs, a lighted cigarette between her lips, reading the evening paper.

If only she had sat anywhere but on the stairs! But no one could get past her and to suggest that she might move aside would be asking for trouble. The only thing to do was to wait. The probationers dispersed and Sister Humby returned to her office, leaving the door ajar to await events.

The time was nearly ten o'clock, and that was when Miss Carlile always retired to bed. Sure enough, as the clock struck the hour, one of the doors opened and the dainty little figure of the sweet-faced, elderly woman passed composedly across the hall to the foot of the stairs, where her way was blocked by the recumbent Mrs. Simpson. Sister Humby craned forward, and saw Miss Carlile bend over the figure at the bottom of the stairs, and heard her say in her gentle, gracious way, "Dear Mrs. Simpson, I'm sure you would not prevent an old woman going up to rest after a busy day."

Mrs. Simpson looked up, hair awry and dark eyes slightly glazed, and some calming influence reached her angry, passionate heart as she looked into the gentle face bent over her. She struggled to her feet, bowed with a flourish, said "Good night, Miss Carlile," and then walked somewhat unsteadily towards the front door. Sister Humby, holding her breath, saw her fumble for the handle, open the door and go out, while Miss Carlile went serenely up the stairs. With a little sigh of relief that was half sigh, half giggle, the warden of the women's work locked the front door and went at last to her bedroom, thankful once more to be free of tormenters. For the tormenters of the Church Army Sisters were a factor to be continually reckoned with, and Sister Humby, who was very young for the responsible position that she held, was repeatedly reminded of their presence and of her own inability to deal with them. Quite apart from individuals like Mrs. Simpson, there was a gang of girls and women of generally dubious reputation, frequenters of public houses, which took special delight in plaguing the Sisters, waylaying them in the dark streets, tweaking the long grey veils they wore, and making themselves such a noisy nuisance in the meetings held in the little chapel at the back of the Church Army headquarters that eventually she had forbidden them entrance altogether. She greatly disliked putting this ban on them, thus excluding them from the meetings which were designed to cater for such as they, but patience with them had been unrewarded and as night after night the little chapel had become the scene of chaos and a babel of voices, she had no option but to make the rule. The Doves as they called themselves, had to content themselves with banging on the windows and singing ribald songs outside in the mews, from which activities they were every now and then moved on by the police.

The contradictory thing about these girls was that although they did their best to make life unendurable for the Sisters, they were up in arms immediately if anybody else tried to do so, and Sister Humby, who was not unconscious of contradictions in herself, had a half-amused, compassionate affection for them, and went to considerable lengths to help any of them in a difficulty. Some of them she knew quite well, finding them easy enough to talk to when unfortified to impertinence by the presence of other Doves. Grace was such a one—slight, fair, with a keen sense of humour and an unexpected compassion for little, helpless creatures. On one occasion, emerging from a public house, she came across a little fledgling sparrow that had fallen from its nest to the hard pavement, and immediately she stopped and picked it up gently, murmuring, "Poor little thing," and marched off with it, cupped in her hands, to the Training College. "Look," she said to Sister Humby, with a challenging look in her eyes, "You're supposed to look after people . . . you look after this poor little bird that's fallen out of its nest!" and as she spoke, she thrust the fledgling into the hands of the warden of women's work. "Mind you let me know if it lives," she said as she departed.

The little fledgling lived. After being carefully fed with rice

38

pudding, it was placed in a basket, and in the middle of the night the Sister heard an excited twittering. Awaking with the fear that the cat had got in, she was just in time to see the mother sparrow flying out of the window, the baby bird on its wings. The moving little climax of the mother-bird's love that sought and found her babe was duly related to Grace. It would have been a most satisfying sequel if she had been sufficiently touched by this episode to change her ways, at least to the extent of refraining from tormenting the very people to whom she instinctively turned for help for the helpless. The fact is, however, that she continued just as before, and with the rest of The Doves was banned from the chapel when evangelistic meetings were in progress.

Sister Humby sensed that there was one of the probationers at least who did not approve of this ban. This new probationer, Sister Gemmel, was several years older than the majority of probationers, although with her happy, vivacious manner and eager participation in all the activities of the college, everyone forgot it. She was always ready to take more than her full share of the chores, although it was evident that previous experience had not run along the lines of domestic work. The first time she was put on the duty of buttering the bread for tea she was discovered cheerfully plastering it on so thick that the Sister-in-charge ejaculated, "Sister dear, I'm afraid we shall soon be in the work-house if we have bread buttered like that!" Her family was obviously well-to-do, and very solicitous of her well-being. Her mother in particular came quite frequently to enquire privately about her health, and the appearance of a small boil caused some alarm. Sister Humby casually remarked that probably Sister Gemmel's blood was out of order, and she needed a little more fruit. The next day a crate of oranges was delivered at the college sufficient for all the Sisters, and to the surprise and amusement of the staff.

With such a background it was surprising, Sister Humby reflected, that this unusual probationer should be so drawn to The Doves. Drawn she certainly was, and on occasion absented herself entirely from the evangelistic meetings to walk round and round, up and down, with one or another of the girls who was forbidden to enter the chapel. "They are so very lonely," she said, and added wistfully, "If only we could give them friendship, not only at the service, but at other times, to show them the love of God." If there was a streak of implied criticism at a failure in love and faith in the remark, Sister Humby was not offended. She understood how this eager recruit felt, for she felt it herself on occasion, that sense of falling short in reaching those who were beyond the pale of respectability. There were times when she would gladly have walked out of the college with its multitudinous demands and its relentless routine, to spend time penetrating through the labyrinthine mental paths of some abandoned woman's mind to the heart whose sensitivity was numbed but not yet dead. She knew where her duty lay, however, and could only look, not go, after those reckless young women walking so defiantly on the very edge of the precipice.

If Sister Humby could not go to them herself, she was glad enough that there was someone who not only could, but who wanted to, and sometimes she would say to one of the girls who was bent on making a nuisance of herself, "You go for a walk with Sister Gemmel." And she observed that although they drew faces, or made pert remarks, or adopted an attitude of complete indifference, they nevertheless went, to the relief of those conducting the meetings and, she hoped to the benefit of the girls themselves.

The young warden of women's work did not pin her hopes of bringing these wild girls to Christ only on the outward and visible contacts made with them, however, She knew that without an inner and invisible contact they would never be fundamentally changed, and she was not aiming at mere moral reformation. So, as the ever-present problem of The Doves was discussed in the College, a suggestion was made which was to have far-reaching effects on Doreen's own service in years to come.

It was a very simple suggestion—merely that each of the probationers should pray regularly for one of The Doves. Their names were listed, and a name given to each of the trainees. One of The Doves was a girl named Ethel, who weighed about sixteen

40

stone. There was an evening when she had been sufficiently influenced at an evangelistic meeting to make her way to the front where an ardent worker knelt beside her and prayed warmly for 'this wee lamb'. The influence of the meeting apparently faded from Ethel, but the appellation stuck, and from that time she was known by all the probationers as 'the wee lamb'. Not without a smile did Doreen receive 'the wee lamb' as her special prayer topic, but she prayed for her faithfully each day, although she knew little about her at this time.

That the new probationer had a deep compassion for 'the wild girls' was noticed by others beside the warden of women's work, and she was amazed a few years later, in a parish in the north of England, when a Church Army Captain greeted her with the remark, "You're the Sister who did so much for those girls at Marble Arch, aren't you?" She herself was quite unaware that she had any unusual measure of interest in The Doves, far less that others felt she was doing anything for them. They were then but an adjunct of the entirely new world in which she found herself, which was satisfying her as nothing else had ever done.

I now began a time which as I look back I know to be nearer Heaven than I shall ever be again on earth. One realizes through such an experience what the world would be like were it Christian. It was one of the busiest times I have ever lived through and yet what a deep peace and sense of serenity brooded over and infiltrated those busy days. The hardest thing to me was still the getting up early—I had never been used to early rising. It had never been a strong point in our family. But gradually I got used to that 6.30 bell, so much so that a few of us asked our Sister-in-charge if we might rise half an hour earlier and go through Hyde Park on those lovely summer mornings.

The powerful influence of the body of men and women amongst whom she had come had its effect on her outlook on mundane affairs. Like Brother Lawrence they saw in every ordinary duty of normal living an opportunity to please God, and as she washed

41

dishes and dusted chairs this thought of doing it for Him gave her a deep sense of pleasure. The well-regulated communal life which to some can be so irksome, to her was extremely satisfying. It prevented her from frittering away time in fruitless day-dreams or inefficient pottering, and she went to bed each night with the wholesome consciousness that the day had been well spent. And it was during these training days that she got her first glimpse of Prebendary Carlile himself.

How well I remember it! Every afternoon at two o'clock we used to walk through Headquarters for midday prayers. For the first week or two of my training days the Chief was not at Headquarters, but one day we were told he would be there. We were sitting at the back of the Prayer Room and the door opened from the dining-room and quite a small crowd of people came out. In the midst I saw the grey-haired head of the one I knew must be our Chief and such a thrill of gratitude went through me as I thanked God for the man who had opened up this glorious way of work for us women in the Church of England —and how much he had gone through to open and keep that door open! What patience he had had in pleading and almost forcing the powers that be to see the urgent need of a band of lay men and women who would go forth into the fight and eventually come to be called by that grand old warrior Bishop Winnington-Ingram, 'The spearhead of the Church'.

She was still in the impressionable early stages of her discipleship. when her character was being moulded for future service, and the part this man all unconsciously played in moulding it cannot be assessed. She knew him to be a leader of men, one who by this time was an acknowledged power in the life of the Church of England, yet there was about him such a complete lack of dignified aloofness, such a boyish eagerness, above all such a deep compassion for those who had sunk to the lowest moral depths, that he became her pattern of a true disciple of the Man, Christ Jesus. He was no weakling, as those who opposed and jeered at him in street meetings soon discovered. One of the first things

C.A. trainees had to learn was how to turn disturbers out of meetings. "Firmly—but in such a kindly, smiling manner that you'll still be on friendly terms when you meet in the street, and able to walk along with them arm-in-arm! Remember—Jesus was the *Friend* of publicans and sinners!" It was this utter disregard of the conventional in reaching out to the lost that attracted Doreen, and she wanted to be 'all out' like him.

"Chief," she said to him once, "I'm afraid of becoming respectable again!" In the course of her visiting she had met a woman who remembered her as a child in Liverpool, and who exclaimed, "I used to see you going through the private gardens with your Nannie, in your beautifully laundered white dresses!" then she added words which Doreen never forgot, "Only Jesus could change a little snob like you!" Perhaps it was the fear of that snobbishness rearing its head again which forced the confession from her. "I'm afraid of becoming respectable again!"

The old Chief looked at her with an understanding twinkle in his eye, then tapped her on the shoulder with the stick he carried. "That's right," he said. "Go on being afraid."

Chapter Six

KILBURN LIES to the west of the Edgware Road as it runs from
Marble Arch up through Maida Vale and on towards St. Albans,
and in the days before the Second World War it bore itself with
an air of determined respectability. Its rows and rows of stucco-
fronted houses with asphalted front yards and railed-in areas
might be devoid of trees and flower beds, but a front of lace-
curtained gentility was carefully maintained. If some of them so
far demeaned themselves as to contain furnished 'bed-sitters', they
prided themselves on taking in only city gentlemen or ladies of
independent means. That there were some fallen so low as to
house occupants of a different order there was no denying, but
others shrank away from them, keeping their front gates closed
and all the blinds drawn firmly down after dark.

While Church Army Sisters and Captains did not fit exactly
into the desired category of 'gentlemen' or 'ladies', their association
with the Church made up for the fact that they wore uniform and
apparently had very little leisure. The landlady of a house in one
of the streets who let a bedroom to a certain Sister Gemmel who
had just come to work with the Vicar in Kilburn, graciously
offered her lodger the use of the front room downstairs should
she ever wish to entertain special guests. Into this chilly room with
its stiff, plush-upholstered sofa and uneasy chairs, Doreen did in
fact receive two cousins who drove up to see her one day, arriving
outside the house in a hired Daimler, complete with chauffeur in
livery. Their abiding impression of the place was 'those awful
lace curtains', and they did not come again.

Doreen's own 'bed-sitter' was on the first floor, and from it she
neither had the view of the railway at the back along which rushed
the express to her beloved Scotland, nor the park that lay opposite
the house. She occupied the side room, through whose windows
she looked out on the wall of the next door house, about three

yards away. Nevertheless, she was supremely happy. Her days were full of activities which took her out amongst people in visitation, women's meetings and the like, and she was filled with admiration for the Vicar's wife

> who was a great inspiration to me always. How busy is the life of a vicar's wife who really shares her husband's vision—the vicarage to run, children to care for, meetings to ⌄ responsible for, constant calls on telephone and at the door, and ever those callers who need real personal attention and advice. I thank God for that vicar's wife—truly a saint.

The Vicar himself 'was a really live wire' and a resourceful man too, as she discovered when, knowing her unusual story, he informed her that Hugh Redwood, author of *God in the Slums* was coming to address a meeting. "Unfortunately it's for men only," he added with a twinkle in his eye. But he smuggled her into the church beforehand, and, hidden in the choir stalls, she listened with bated breath to the throaty drawling voice of the man whose writing had altered the course of her life. It was tantalizing to hear him and yet be unable to meet him.

There was only one thing she had against the parish into which she had come—it was too respectable. The new Sister had a taste for the slums, and it was to the under-privileged and the outcasts from society that she was irresistibly drawn. It was not long before she discovered something which respectable Kilburn would fain have kept concealed—a common lodging-house for men.

> Oh, what a place! One went down an ill-lit alley off the main road and came into a courtyard, filled with dustbins and old chairs, a place of mixed odours—dust, stale food, cooking, humanity, etc. Would it be possible to get in? The Vicar gave me permission to ask the owner, so one morning I bearded him in his office. I remember he was a big man with a large sombrero hat, and a fierce-looking Alsatian dog! But both were quite friendly, and I got the necessary permission. So one night I met a few of our keen young people in the chapel and we sallied

forth with our little harmonium. On arrival at the lodging-house we discovered that the owner had forgotten to leave word that we were to be admitted. Nothing daunted, we gathered around the harmonium in a courtyard filled with dustbins. Our congregation that night was made up of heads appearing through windows of neighbouring poor houses and we returned, feeling it had been a night well spent.

The following week we got right inside. Men of all ages were sitting at wooden tables and at one side was a large open range where some were cooking their supper, others were reading, others playing chess. It was no easy work to start a service in such an atmosphere, but as the weeks went by we got some sort of hearing until the night came when I felt we could have a solo, and a lass with a very sweet voice came with us and sang, "Steal away, steal away, steal away to Jesus . . ." There was a wonderful hush as she sang that Negro spiritual.

As she got better known, some of the men would hail her if they met her in the street, and this acknowledgment of her as a friend gave her great satisfaction. One of these men, a tall, thin, bearded fellow, who had at one time been Private Secretary to Lord Rothermere, said he would be willing to go to church if he could get a pair of shoes.

That was easily managed through our clothing department. How good all the other departments in Church Army have been in helping over any problem I ever took to them.

Behind the stucco-fronted terraced houses of Kilburn human tragedies were being lived out, and burrowing beneath the surface Doreen began to feel her way into a subterranean world of sorrow and shame. A popular song of those days ran:

> City of laughter, city of tears
> What are the secrets you hold?
> What are the sorrows beneath the joys
> The pain 'neath the glitter of gold?

And one of the verses ended with the words:

> There are hearts that seem light
> That are breaking tonight
> In that city of laughter and tears.

and in her first week in the parish Doreen found one of them. The Church Army Captain who had been appointed to the parish a month previously had already started a Saturday night 'Pub round', when workers armed with *Church Army Gazettes* for sale went into the public houses of the district to get into contact with the men and women who lounged around the bars, and she enthusiastically entered into this activity. In one of the public houses she spoke to a dark-haired, quite respectable-looking woman who said to her, "I don't like seeing you in these places. You remind me of my daughter, these places aren't for you."

Doreen looked at her and smiled. "I think these are the sort of places my Lord would come to," she said gently, "so that's why I come . . . I wonder . . . could I come and see you sometime? Where do you live? I'd love to visit you."

"Would you?" the woman asked, rather surprised. Her breath smelt strongly of beer, but she was still sober. "My name's Mrs. Hodges . . . you can come and see me if you want to . . ." and she gave her address. Making a note of it Sister Gemmel went on her way, but the memory of the woman's words remained with her—"You remind me of my daughter." Just for a moment a curtain had been drawn aside, revealing a wistful mother's heart, and it was not many days after that the grey uniformed figure of the Sister was standing outside the front door of the house where Mrs. Hodges lived, drawn by the consciousness of human need. But when Mrs. Hodges eventually appeared in response to the shout of the landlady who opened the door, she refused to invite her visitor up to her room on the top storey. "It's too dirty," she said and they only had a brief conversation on the front doorstep that time. When Doreen called again she took a hand brush and a duster with her, and suggested to Mrs. Hodges that they should clean her rooms together.

47

I think this must have spurred her on. She still refused to let me go up, but said she would clean it, and then I could come in. At last the great day came and I was allowed in. I found it quite a nice little flat. Hers was a sad story. Her husband had died, her boy had been killed in the war, and not very long ago her daughter to whom she had been devoted had also died. She was lonely, very lonely and was finding her greatest consolation in drink.

So started the friendship which proved the first link in a chain that drew the lonely drunkard to the One who was known as a Friend of publicans and sinners. It was not the only link. Doreen, knowing the danger of Mrs. Hodges' loneliness, enlisted the sympathetic help of a simple, sincere church member, who would never have summoned up courage enough to go into a public house, but whose heart was touched with compassion as she heard Mrs. Hodges' story. "Yes, I'll meet her and go out for a walk with her," she said willingly.

She did more. Mrs. Hodges was persuaded to attend church socials and on one Saturday evening Sister Gemmel arrived at the hall after doing the 'pub round' to find one in full swing.

"Just a song at twilight, when the lights are low," they were all singing lustily, and glancing over the audience she noticed Mrs. Hodges, and realized that she was none too sober. There was a drawl in her voice as she crooned the popular song which gave her away, and Doreen decided it would be wise to persuade her to go home, where she would not disgrace herself publicly. Gently she wormed her way alongside the woman, and suggested home and bed. Mrs. Hodges was amenable enough, and the two of them set out along the respectable Kilburn streets, the grey-clad Sister arm in arm with a woman who reeled somewhat as she walked, and burst out every now and again into the "song at twilight". The rooms she occupied were filthy, and there were about fifteen empty beer bottles lying around on the floor. It took Doreen some time to get her safely in bed, and when there she continued singing. The song at twilight, the flickering shadows, the lights that are low, the day that is long were rather confused, but ended with a triumphant conclusion in love's old sweet song. And at last Mrs. Hodges slept.

Rome was not built in a day, and neither are those who have wandered out of the way easily sought and found. It was not until the following year, when Sister Gemmel had left Kilburn and was working in a parish in Durham, that Mrs. Hodges, at a large meeting, conducted by Prebendary Carlile himself, responded to his invitation to any present who desired to follow Christ to stand and repeat the words, "Lord, Thou knowest that I love Thee," and started life anew.

On my return to London the following year I went to see her. What a transformation! It would have been possible to eat one's food off her shining polished floor, and my mind went back to the floor as I used to know it. She was still in the same parish and had been so safely cared for and shepherded by faithful workers there. How much we owe to those who so quietly and conscientiously work behind the scenes for love of God. After the beginning of Bethany she never failed to send me 10/- out of her pension every Christmas. It was one January afternoon as I sat in my little office writing to thank her that from our big room, which I had lent for a party, came the strains of a song. I laid down my pen and listened—yes, and wept. It was 'Just a song at twilight . . .' How I thanked God for His redeeming and restoring love.

Although Kilburn is some distance from Marble Arch, even here she was brought in touch with The Doves, and the manner in which it happened is not without significance. She had been to Bloomsbury to speak at a Christian Endeavour meeting, and although she was tired after a busy day, and was ready enough to mount a bus and head for home, she felt strangely impelled not to do so, but rather to walk. So strong was the conviction that she started off towards Oxford Street on foot. She had walked the length of it, right up to Marble Arch, and was just turning into Edgware Road when she saw one of the gang running towards her.

"Oh, Sister," she panted. "Do speak to Ethel. She's got nowhere to sleep tonight . . ." Ethel! Ethel of all people! Doreen knew the name well, for Ethel was the name of the girl allotted to her to pray for while she was still in the Training College. Eagerly she went forward to where Ethel stood on the pavement, a huge figure of indifference mingled with despair. She did not care, she said. She was used to 'sleeping rough'. And as Sister Gemmel walked around the streets with her that night, she got what was perhaps her first glimpse into the subterranean world of a great city— the world, not of lurid night-clubs and exciting exotic dens conjured in the imaginations of those who know nothing about it, but the world of the outcasts who drift from seats in the parks to the platforms of railway termini, only to be 'moved on' by the police; who know the whereabouts of derelict buildings and warehouses into which they can sneak when it rains, and lie there; the flotsam and jetsam of humanity that has 'no fixed address', that spends a few nights in this cheap lodging-house, a few nights there, 'sleeping rough' when money has run out, going into the public lavatories early in the morning to get a quick wash, suspiciously viewed by the attendant, before emerging to face life in the daylight as best they can.

Ethel had been turned out of her home when she was sixteen. Not without cause had her mother implacably shut the front door on her, for she had brought disgrace on the family from quite an early age, making her way up to Hyde Park to loiter and trifle with the soldiers who lounged there, and would brook no restraint. Nevertheless, home always drew her—it was where she belonged. When the night came in which, for the first time, the door was closed to her, therefore, the shock of it went deep. Too proud to beg admittance and apologize, she turned away not knowing where to go, and started walking around the streets. Midnight came and passed and still she wandered round, defiant, hurt, numbed with the knowledge that the door of home was shut. At 2 o'clock it started to rain. She walked on, till she saw the lights of an all-night garage. There were two or three men inside and they called to her.

"Come in 'ere out o' the rain, sweetie . . ."

"Out late ter night arn't yer? we'll find room for yer here . . ."

She caught her breath as she looked at their inquisitive, appraising eyes, scanning her boldly. This was different from the merry flirtations in the park, which had led on to careless intimacy, and she knew it. But it was raining, she had nowhere to go, and "It doesn't matter. Nobody cares," she thought recklessly. So she went in.

"Got me started that night," she told Doreen with an oath, expecting to shock her. "Don't you worry about me, Sister," she continued. "I know my way around, all right. Huh! Don't you worry . . . !"

But Doreen did worry. The thought of the great, desperate, defiant girl came again and again, and the sense of the underlying loneliness and despair. She could not forget. She kept in touch with her, all unconsciously beginning to fulfil her own longing to "show them the love of God"—that love which is patient and suffers long and goes on being kind.

Chapter Seven

DOREEN WAS restless. She did not know why but there was an underlying dissatisfaction in her mind which she realized was increasing. She had been in Kilburn for nearly two years, and although she found work in the parish congenial enough, she felt she could not spend the rest of her life in a round of visitation of Church members, running women's meetings, serving on committees to organize bazaars and the like. There was a pent-up energy of soul which was not finding an outlet, an unorthodoxy which could not conform to convention. At that time open-air meetings with hymn singing and short sermons were conducted weekly in some of the streets, and she observed that very few people stopped to listen. If only they could collect a crowd! She remembered the remark that had once been made to her by an old Church Army worker, who, in spite of her elastic-sided boots and a generally slap-dash appearance, was a fervent and effective evangelist. "My dear, it doesn't matter how you get a crowd as long as you get them. You can get a crowd anyhow—just take a tray and bang it in the street, and people will come, and then you can preach to them!" Bring a tray and get a crowd—that was the idea!

She suggested to the Vicar that she and the Church Army Captain attached to the church should adopt this method, and without thought he agreed. When she brought the matter up at the regular Monday morning staff meeting, however, hoping to get on with the arrangements, the Vicar looked rather perturbed.

"You know, I don't really think you can do that," he said uneasily, fearful that in his respectable parish such an exhibition would eventually deter more than it would attract, and create uncomfortable disturbances in the Parochial Church Council meetings.

"But you *said* we could!" remonstrated the disappointed Sister.

"I'm sorry," replied the Vicar firmly, "I'm sorry, but I really don't think I can let you do that . . ."

It was to the Vicar later on, that she confided her feeling of restlessness, and the unfortunate man, with typical masculine inability to understand a woman's feelings, made a remark which proved fatal as far as retaining this popular Sister in his parish was concerned.

"Oh, you'll be all right when the warm weather comes and you can play tennis!" he said indulgently. "That's what you need!"

If he sensed that his observation had upset rather than pacified her, he probably put it down to feminine unreasonableness, and decided that what she really needed was to be married. He would have been genuinely distressed had he known that she was walking along the roads of respectable Kilburn in a frame of mind alternating between indignation and bewilderment at what he had said.

Tennis! 'You'll be all right when the warm weather comes and you can play tennis!' Who wants to play tennis, she thought. She hadn't joined the Church Army to play tennis! She could play tennis at home, and get a much better game there than in Kilburn, anyhow! Tennis! She strode to a telephone, and got through to the Church Army Headquarters, and asked to speak to Miss Carlile. She wanted to see her, she said, to talk things over with her.

On the day appointed she went for the interview, back to the familiar, loved Headquarters of Church Army, and into the little office where Miss Carlile awaited her, her soft, grey veil hanging down round her gentle face. And there, with one whom she could trust, and who she knew would thoroughly understand, she poured out her unreasonable indignation. Tennis! Who wanted to go in for mere amusements? Feel better when she could play tennis!

The older woman listened patiently. With her quick insight she recognized that there was some deeper cause for this disquiet of soul than either Doreen or the Vicar knew, and when the outburst expended itself, she quietly tried to explain the man's point of view and then added:

"You'd better go away and think and pray about it." Perhaps the week's rest would ease the nervous tension under which this unusual young Sister was living, and in the meantime a sphere could be found for her which she would find more congenial.

The week's rest did little to relieve Doreen's mind—she felt as unsettled as before. Then she heard from Headquarters that it had been decided to send her to work among fisher girls in Scotland. She was Scottish herself, and the appointment seemed very suitable. Moreover, the Church Army Sister in charge of the area where the fisher girls work was carried on was delighted, saying that she had felt Sister Gemmel to be the one for this work for a long time. There seemed no reason to doubt that this was the niche into which Sister Gemmel would fit most readily, and she did not doubt it herself until one Sunday morning, back in her lodgings in Kilburn, sitting by the fire while her landlady laid her breakfast, she was dismayed at an imperative command which came to her mind with such unexpected clarity that she did not doubt it came from God.

"Go up to Headquarters and tell them you are not to go!"

The words were so distinct that she looked round, almost expecting to see someone. No one was there, but that command was insistent. "Go up to Headquarters and tell them you are not to go."

"But how can I?" she argued in dismay. Everything was arranged, she was all set to go to Scotland. How foolish and unreasonable she would look if she went now to say that she could not go because God had told her not to! How could she make anyone understand, how explain that imperative command which rang so clearly in her mind, but not, apparently, in anyone else's? No, she must go through with things now, she decided miserably. All she could do was to pray rather desperately that God would overrule.

Their is no other explanation for what happened then but that God did indeed overrule. Unaccountably, a few days later, her arm swelled just below the shoulder. She went to the doctor who sent her immediately to the Middlesex Hospital for an X-ray. There was no evident reason for that swelling. She was sent home for a rest, and went first to her mother in Liverpool, then up to Aunt Peg at Kilmacolm. The arm was still swollen, though without pain, and no diagnosis of the doctors seemed to tally; it was never finally diagnosed. Eventually the swelling went down, and she returned to Kilburn. The matter of work among the fisher girls faded out.

Then it was suggested that she should move to a parish in the north, in the mining district of County Durham. This time everything went smoothly. The parishioners in Kilburn presented her with a beautiful picture of Christ in Gethsemane (which in years to come was to adorn the walls of Bethany) and at the close of evensong on the last Sunday she was there the Vicar asked her to come forward.

"We want to ask God's blessing on our Sister as she leaves us to go to her new appointment in Felling," he said, and as she knelt at the communion rail, and heard the sweeping rustle of the large congregation kneeling also, listened to the Vicar simply and reverently addressing himself to God on her behalf, she knew herself enveloped in a wave of prayer and sympathy. With assurance and a sense of embarking on another divine adventure she set off for the north.

. . . where, of course, I was quite at home. I never really felt strange for a moment among the folk at Felling. I think I loved them from the very beginning. How patient they were with me! I shall ever be grateful for their help and understanding. My first Vicar used to 'tremble' when I brought out my little notebook with all its requests—lodging-houses, pubs, etc. Well, it was quite soon that this little book began to be in action with my second Vicar. I asked for an evening meeting for women, as many were untouched and were just sitting out on their doorsteps at night in the back alley behind the Mission Church. He gave me permission, bless him, and God blessed this venture. We began with fifteen, and two years later, when I left, we had eighty-one.

The little notebook was produced at another staff meeting,

this time with a request concerning public house visitation.

I don't think there was a second's hesitation in the Vicar's mind, and he gladly said yes. But a little later, I was told that someone said I was bringing the Church into disrepute. It was the Vicar himself who told me, and I said to him as I had said to Mrs. Hodges, that I believed the Lord would have me there. I so truly believe in Luke v. 32. Anyway had got the I permission, so the next thing was to call on the publicans and that proved to be a very joyful job! All gave me permission, only one refused (a Presbyterian!) and a few weeks later the only one I had not called on, a Roman Catholic, sent for me to come to his pub, too, to sell Church Army *Gazettes*!

One Saturday night (I remember it had just begun to snow) an old lady named Johnson came up to me in the dark and said, "My old man's ill. He told me, if I saw you, to ask if you would come in and pray with him." I did not know her or her old man, but evidently they sat in the public house and had seen me going in every Saturday night and now that he was ill his thoughts had turned God-wards, and I was the only one who came to his mind as having anything to do with God.

Gladly she responded to the request, and discovered to her surprise that the elderly couple were living on a new housing estate in a comfortable little house, complete with bathroom. The bathroom was never used for the purpose intended, but came in very useful as a place to dump things in and it was from here that a dilapidated Bible was produced when the Sister asked for one. The old man, who had cancer, started to read it and learned the 23rd Psalm off by heart, resting his fears at last as he put his trust in the Shepherd of the Psalm. And his wife, restive and nervy at first when Sister Gemmel visited them, gradually quietened down, started attending church services and was eventually confirmed.

The neighbours wondered what had happened to that home— the quarrelling and swearing had ceased to be.

56

Her influence in the public house community was observed by those most likely to benefit by it—the wives of the frequenters. "You know Sister," one of the members of her Sunshine Circle said to her, "our men tell us that all the filthy stories and swearing stop while you are in the pub."

If the Vicar of Felling had occasion from such experiences to be grateful for the new Church Army Sister in his parish, everything she did was not so successful. It was very disturbing for instance to receive a visit from a father who came to complain about the lack of discipline now at the Sunday meeting known as the Children's Church. When Sister Gemmel took it over, the behaviour of the eighty odd children who attended it was exemplary—now look at them! The Vicar, a kind-hearted man, looked very worried as he told her of this complaint, for he shrank from saying anything that would wound a fellow worker. But the matter could not be ignored. "Something will have to be done about it," he said.

It was a humiliating experience, but as with all such, when taken in the right spirit, it produced good results, not only in the work, but also in the character of the still immature Sister.

An attractive personality, a ready smile and an equally ready wit might ensure her an entry and a hearing in public houses, but evidently something more, something which she lacked, was required to control children. She went back to her lodgings with an acute sense of shame and an even more acute sense of failure. The work which had been commenced and so successfully run by her predecessor was now in danger of being ruined by her bungling inexperience. And there was nothing she could do about it. She had no training in dealing with children, she had never even been to Sunday School as a child herself. She had no resources, and almost in desperation she got down on her knees and prayed.

"Oh, God!" she said urgently, "I *can't* manage these children. I don't know how to. Oh, God, if *You* don't do something that Children's Church will have to be closed. Oh, Lord, please will *You* do something."

How it happened she did not know—indeed it happened so imperceptibly that she was quite unaware that her prayer was being answered until one Sunday evening she suddenly realized that now the children came in cheerfully, happily, without rush or rowdiness, and that when she mounted the platform, they immediately quietened down, looking up at her expectantly, ready to respond to whatever lead she gave. God had answered her prayer. Just what He had done or how He had done it she did not know, but as she watched the 'sidesmen' take up the collection, listening to the clatter of coppers rattling in the biscuit tin lids that served as collection plates, and sat without strain and tension in the friendly relaxed atmosphere, she knew that it was God Who had taken control. The number of children had nearly doubled by the time she left Felling to return to a different type of work in London, and she did not know when or how the increase had come about. What she did know was that in some mysterious way God had entered into a situation that was beyond her, that He had done it after she had cried to Him and not before, and that although it now appeared to be her presence that commanded the attention of the children, it really was not so at all. Another was in control, and the only reason everybody did not realize it was merely because she, not He, was the one they saw.

Chapter Eight

SISTER GEMMEL was not cut out for parish work—at any rate, that was how she felt about it. "I'm not respectable enough for a parish," she said again and again, and with her constant bent towards the unusual and the unorthodox, that instinct which drew her inevitably to the outcast and the misfit, it would not have been surprising if her hard-pressed Vicar had agreed with her. "This must be one of your friends—it couldn't be anyone else's!" someone had said to her at a church social, indicating a woman who had found her way in a little the worse for drink. Sure enough, it *was* one of her friends! When she had been in Felling for two years and the same restlessness which had disturbed her at Kilburn assailed her, however, the Vicar was genuinely reluctant to let her go. But the observant leaders of Church Army work at Marble Arch recognized in her qualities which would fit her for a new type of evangelism which the agile-minded Chief, now in his eighty-ninth year, was about to launch. Ever eager to enrol the layman into active service for his Master, he now had the aim of establishing a 'News Team' in every parish —a little group of people who would be prepared to mount the chancel steps in churches and tell out, in simple, direct manner, what the living Christ had done for them. To head up the women's teams a Church Army Sister was needed, and the one chosen was Doreen Gemmel. So back to London she went, to share a flat with two other Sisters. Within easy access of Head-quarters, she added to the peace of mind of her mother in Liverpool by getting her midday meal there. "At least she'll have one decent meal," that lady sighed thankfully. Her daughter had no flair for housekeeping.

There was a tree outside the room Doreen occupied in the flat, and before she donned her uniform and set out for the duties of the day, she used to kneel by her window praying, opening her eyes every now and then to rest them on the soft green of the leaves. She loved the beauties of nature, and perhaps the greatest privation of which she was conscious in her years lived in the heart of the world's greatest city was the separation from them. "Sometimes the beauty of the earth brings a lump in my throat," she wrote once. "And yet I am so glad to be living here for His sake. I put up the picture of a hill or a tree—they help to lift my thoughts above the things of the world."

The sordid side of the world certainly revealed itself aggressively as she found herself from time to time at the evening meetings in the little chapel in the mews behind the Headquarters' building. The Doves still continued to force their way in, often drunk, and would shout, heckle and even fight each other there when they had a quarrel among themselves. It was at this time that they forced themselves into Sister Gemmel's consciousness as never before, so that even when she was away on News Team work her thoughts flew to them. The inarticulate cry of their defiantly-covered need would not be silenced.

"They're lonely," she said to the Chief, and he, ever alive to the claims of the outcast, listened sympathetically to her. "They want *friendship*. We don't really know them at all." Together they discussed some way of meeting this need, and even went so far as to suggest at a staff meeting that the chapel should be used one night a week as a sort of club-room for the gang, where they could come and play some games, and have a cup of tea. Prebendary Carlile had a great faith in the value of a cup of tea. "It breaks barriers and loosens tongues," he said, "people will talk over a cup of tea, and then they'll even listen, and then's our chance! A lesser sacrament it can be, a cup of tea!" The suggestion that the chapel should be used for such a purpose was rejected, not unwisely, by the staff, and the old Chief, who never forced his way through against his colleagues' convictions, did not press the matter further. But Doreen sensed his disappointment that there still seemed no way of extending the hand of human fellowship for these wild outcasts, and felt a glow of satisfaction that he and she were on the same side, even though it was the losing side.

I think it must have been at this stage that I felt the call of the outcast even as the Chief knew it. As there seemed no opening to touch my 'Hyde Park gang' I felt God meant me to do more for these deep down in the roadway of life, especially as I had been led to Him by a book that told of the slums. A vital part of this story lies in the Sisters who were in training this summer term of 1936. Many years afterwards I was to discover that a few of them decided to get up half an hour earlier every morning to pray for this little gang. I always say *they* were the ones who caused Bethany to be born, because it was just at this time that God so laid these folk on my heart, and it seemed so clear to me that all their playing-up was caused through loneliness, and their completely indescribable behaviour at times was caused through their determination to get attention paid to themselves, *however* they got it. 'Noticitis' we call it in Bethany!

And so it was, in 1936, that she made her specific request to be allowed to work among the 'down-and-outs', and to have a little room allocated to her where they could always come, at any time of the day and night, and be assured of a welcome. Reluctant to lose her from the News Team work, the Chief did not acquiesce immediately, but it was so evident where her heart was that eventually she was given permission to begin as soon as a little room suitable for the purpose could be found.

Then weeks passed, and nothing happened. She was still connected with the News Team work, and no little room had materialized. One Monday morning, kneeling by her window, she had a sense of urgency about it. Something must be done. She could not go on and on waiting for something to happen, while those girls were drifting more and more rapidly downstream. But until the room was provided, she could not make a start.

"Oh, Lord!" she prayed suddenly, almost violently. "Oh, Lord, if You want me to do this work, *please show me a room*!"

It was while she was sitting in her little office that morning that a message came to her from the Sister in charge of the Women's Hostels Department. Could Sister Gemmel go and see her at two o'clock that afternoon? Expecting that she was required to

61

arrange for a Women's News Team to visit the hostels, she went all unsuspecting and knocked at the office door. "Come in," called Sister Brookfield, and then, as Doreen entered, she said, "I think we have found a room for you. Will you come and see it with me?"

"I think we have found a room for you!" Was she hearing aright? She could scarcely believe it was true.

How great was my lack of faith! I had asked Him for it a few hours before and then was surprised at these wonderful, never-to-be-forgotten words, 'I think we have found a room for you!' The one who spoke them lived very close to God and was a woman of much prayer, and I knew she would really be saying, 'I think *He* has found a room for you.'

The room was about ten minutes' walk from Marble Arch, and was attached to one of the Women's Hostels in a turning off the Edgware Road. Above it was another room which Sister Gemmel could have as her own bedroom—so now she could settle in, spend all day and all night, if need be, gathering her outcasts around her.

Joyfully she made her arrangements. Her antique bureau, a chest of drawers, a bookcase, a wardrobe, a gate-legged table and a couple of chairs comprised her personal furniture, and an aunt sent her a cheque 'towards a bed'. A newly acquired sense of economy resulted in her obtaining not only a bed, but an umbrella as well, with the money. At last she was to have her heart's desire, aptly expressed in the little rhyme:

> Let me live in a house by the side of the road
> And be a friend to man.

The house where her room was situated was indeed by the side of the road, and a road with a bad reputation at that. Nothing could be better, from her point of view. Public houses and houses of ill-fame were the sort of places into which those she was seeking were likely to drift, and their presence presented no obstacle. She would open her room, she decided, on the second Saturday in October, and the first person she would bring into it should be Grace.

What might have discouraged her, had she known it, was the attitude of the very girls she sought towards her. "Want no truck with her!" they said. They were not going to be patronized, least of all by one whom, with refined speech and manner, they considered a snob.

"Come on, Elsie," said Grace to her sister one day. "Don't have anything to do with her. She's like our Rose," and then she added violently, "She's stuck up!"

Chapter Nine

IT WAS the first Saturday in October 1936. In another week, thought Doreen, as she set out the cups and saucers in her little bed-sitting room in Bendall Street, the room below would be opened at last, and her work amongst her girls really started in earnest. She had invited one of the other Sisters to tea with her today, but next week she would be preparing for Grace. And she knew she would have to go and get her out of the public house first!

Next week. There were only seven more days to wait now, but this afternoon she found herself unaccountably disturbed at the prospect of the delay. It was as though some alarm had suddenly been sounded, alerting her. She sat and chatted with her friend, but all the time there was that insistent sense of imminent danger, and in the middle of the conversation she broke off what she was saying to exclaim:

"You know, I believe I ought not to wait till next Saturday. I believe I ought to go and find Grace tonight. I'll have time after we get back from the News Team in Islington to go round for her before the pubs close."

"All right," said her friend readily. "I'll come with you if you like. Where do you think she'll be?"

"At the New Inn," replied Doreen with certainty. "She'll be there from opening time till it closes. She's there every night."

But Grace was not at the New Inn nor, it appeared, had she been there all the evening. Doreen returned to her room with the silent alarm disturbing her more than ever. Years later she learned how fateful were those hours, and how the whole course of Grace's life was at stake that week-end.

Grace was a drunkard, and walking recklessly near to a precipice of which she was aware, but over which she had not yet slipped. She was not in London's underworld, although she knew of its existence, and it was not without a sinister fascination for her. She said to herself sometimes, "If I once get mixed up with the underworld, I'm finished. It'll get me . . .." And some inward restraint, some Divine preservation, the outcome surely of her godly mother's prayers, had prevented her hitherto. But on that fateful Saturday, when Doreen was conscious of sudden alarm, Grace met a man who took her, not into a public house with its ribald, cheerful atmosphere, but into a room underground, entered by a door in a dimly lit street, where there was a baneful air of secrecy, and where Grace, incautious as she was, felt slightly uneasy. People there were drinking liquor out of enamel jugs instead of the usual tumblers, and the room was almost deliberately repellent in its dinginess, as though abnormality were encouraged. She knew she was on the very fringe of the underworld, and that the man had a motive in bringing her to this place. He was 'sizing her up'. When he parted from her that night they had arranged to meet again on the following Wednesday.

All her life Grace remembered that night. It was not only the experience of finding herself being drawn to the purlieu of that hidden world of crime and vice that impressed her mind, but the strange sense she had of being followed.

"I seemed to feel footsteps behind me all the time," she told Sister Gemmel years later. "Even when I went down into that room I seemed to feel them. It was as though Someone was following me, coming after me, to get me back."

> But with unhurrying chase,
> And unperturbèd pace,
> Deliberate speed, majestic instancy,
> They beat—and a Voice beat
> More instant than the Feet—
> 'All things betray thee, who betrayest Me'.

So had Francis Thompson written decades before, and so did Grace know the experience of those following Footsteps on this first Saturday in October 1936. But Doreen knew nothing about all this. She had responded with a thrill of joy to the challenge contained in the little chorus:

> *Christ has no hands but our hands*
> *To do His work today,*
> *He has no feet but our feet . . .*

but she little realized how literally hers had to be the feet with which He should follow Grace. She only knew the sense of urgency which impelled her, having failed to find Grace on Saturday, to go and seek for her again on Sunday.

This time she had no difficulty in finding her. Grace was in her usual haunt, at the New Inn, and Doreen, standing outside, sent a message in telling her someone wanted to speak to her. In a minute or two Grace appeared, her face flushed, her hair tousled.

"I'm in the middle of a drink," she said angrily, glaring at the Sister.

"Well, go back and finish it," replied Doreen cheerfully. "Then come along—I've got something to tell you." Grace went back, finished her drink, had another, and eventually emerged in a frame of mind which, to say the least of it, was not co-operative.

"What do you want?" she demanded irritably.

"Grace," said Sister Gemmel gently. "I've got a little room. It's a little room that you can come to any time of the day or night, a little room where you'll always be welcome, a little room that you can call 'home'."

"And what do I want with a little room?" asked Grace. "A little room! Huh! What good's a little room going to do me?"

The portents were not encouraging, and had Doreen been alone Grace might have slipped through her fingers. Another Sister had come with her, however, and talking persuasively the two of them slipped their arms through those of the reluctant woman and propelled her slowly along the Edgware Road to Bendall Street.

The little room certainly did not present a very homelike appearance, for it was not yet properly furnished, the night was cold, and there was no coal with which to make a fire. Grace, strangely enough, did not seem to mind, and gradually her mood changed. She started talking, telling Doreen more about herself than ever before. She didn't want to be like she was, she said, but she didn't know how to be different. She wanted to, but she couldn't.

Doreen sat silent, quietly listening. She knew that this girl, unlike herself, had started life in a Christian home. There was nothing she had not heard about Christ's power to save. 'Gospel-hardened' was Grace, and Doreen felt there was little she could say that would touch her now. The love of Christ must be revealed in deeds rather than in words to such as she.

It was after midnight when they had a cup of hot Oxo together, and Grace was ready to depart. "Come and see me again next Saturday," said Sister Gemmel.

"Yes," said Grace slowly, looking at her. "Next Saturday . . . And what am I going to do on Monday, Tuesday, Wednesday, Thursday, Friday . . . ? I'm going back to those friends of mine, and they're going to say 'What a fool you are to have anything to do with the Church Army! Why don't you live your life and have a good time while you can . . .?' Next Saturday!"

Doreen knew nothing about that appointment made for Wednesday night. Reason told her that Grace had been living as she was for years, and one more week would make little difference. But the words, "I'm going back to those friends of mine . . ." forced themselves upon her attention. Again there came that indefinable sense of urgency.

"Grace," she retorted promptly. "You're not going back to those friends of yours. You're *not* going back to those friends of yours. You're not going back to that lodging-house tonight, even. You're going to stay here. I've got a camp bed, and I'm going to put it up here for you, and tomorrow I'm going to arrange for you to stay in one of our hostels, and you're never going back to the old life."

Long after Grace was sleeping soundly on the camp bed Sister Gemmel, awake in the room above, was making her plans for the day that lay ahead, and in the morning she told Grace what she would do.

I got her to write a note giving me permission to bring everything away from that lodging-house. I first went to our Clothing Department, where I bought a hat box for eight-pence. (That hat box was still being used by Grace ten years afterwards as a coal box.) So I set off for Islington. When I arrived at the lodging-house they kindly gave me everything. I had a suitcase with a lock off, the hat box full to bursting, and a coat over my arm, when they brought up a plate, a saucepan and a frying pan! These were wrapped in a greasy piece of newspaper, and I set off.

As she walked along the street, laden with Grace's belongings, she suddenly caught a glimpse of herself, reflected in a shop window.

What an apparition! Just for a moment I hoped folk would not think it was a Sister moving from one parish to another, and pride reared its head again. I knew that had that pride still been within me in all the strength and force of the old days, I would never, never have 'lowered myself', first of all to enter a common lodging-house, and secondly to look the sight I looked that day.

As swiftly as came the surge of shame there came a subduing thought which put the shame to flight. She remembered that Jesus had been known as a friend of publicans and sinners—not a benefactor, not a helper, not one who patronized them, but a friend, and that He had reminded His followers, "I am among you as one that serveth."

What a privilege to look just not quite respectable if a soul was going to be helped to climb up to the heights from a way that was gradually, but very surely, leading her down to the depths! And so for ever Grace turned her back on common lodging-houses and underworld clubs. What a great help another Sister was in those first few weeks of Grace's early days at Bethany. She would take her out to lunch, she would chat with her, she gave her friendship. At night-time Grace slept in our Hostel at the White Hart, Waterloo. What it must have meant to many a weary soul to lie down in a place so steeped in prayer, and how appropriate it was that the hostel was a converted pub! The Doves were enraged about this capture of one of their flock. Grace's sister Elsie came to me one night very angry. How dare I take her sister away from her? I gently showed her that nothing like that was happening—she could meet her sister any time in the little room, but if I could possibly help it, never again in a public house. By now it was midnight, so I suggested we had a cup of tea together. This suggestion was rather grudgingly accepted and, as usual, barriers were broken down and we parted friends.

The reformation of Grace was by no means complete, even after she got a good 'living-in' job as a domestic servant, and she continued drinking for years. But she was loyal to Sister Gemmel. With her first week's wages she bought a red chenille table-cloth and presented it to her. Deeply touched, Doreen remonstrated, "You shouldn't spend your money on me!" "Better you have it than the publican, isn't it?" demanded Grace gruffly. But there were many times when the publican did get it, and as the weeks passed Doreen realized that Grace's visits to Bethany were frequently interspersed with visits to the public house around the corner, and that the money the girl could have used to establish herself in a self-respecting manner of life was, instead, supplying her with that which degraded her. She would be better off without that money in her handbag, thought Sister as she stood with her back to the door of Bethany, a furious Grace before her trying to get out 'and have a quick one'. It was after a few such tussles that she conceived the plan which was to become an integral and effective feature of Bethany. The next time Grace arrived slightly the worse for drink and put her handbag on the sofa, Sister Gemmel promptly sat on it. Later on she deliberately opened the handbag, took out all the money that was in it, selected a few small coins and carefully returned them, pocketing the rest.

"I'm going to open a Post Office Savings Bank account for you, Grace," she said.

"What a cheek!" replied Grace, taken aback.

"I don't care if it is a cheek," replied Doreen. "I'm going to put the money in the Post Office for you, and what's more I'm going to keep the book." She was as good as her word. Every time Grace came along with a week's wages in her bag she demanded part of it, and in spite of protestations and arguments, the money was handed over. In the years to come she was to be a regular visitor to the Post Office in Great Cumberland Place, opening Post Office Savings accounts with the money she obtained from members of the Bethany family. One of them observed laughingly:

"It has its funny side, for on becoming one of this family you are nagged to death until you get a Post Office book, and it's as safe as the Bank of England once you hand it over—you just get it when you *need* it, not when you want it! I've tried on more than one occasion to get it away—I've given up now, I just give her the money!" But then came the admission:

"What it's meant, that someone cared enough to make me pay in and to hold that book for me! And I have to give thanks to God she has had it, for it's been needed on more than one occasion to get me straight . . ." At one time Sister Gemmel had in her possession eighteen Post Office Savings Bank books, and to the eighteen people to whom they belonged, some of them women who had spent many years in prison, Bethany was 'home', the one place in the world they could go to and always be sure of a welcome.

In the autumn of 1936, however, although several other members of the gang came to Bethany, Grace was the only one whose manner of life had changed at all. At least she was established in a living-in domestic job in a decent home.

But even her reformation was such an uncertain affair that when New Year's Night drew near Doreen was filled with apprehension lest the girl should break out again; lest that fatal consciousness of loneliness should overwhelm her on the night of gaiety, and drive her to seek again the conviviality of the public house. But on this occasion, as on so many others, Violet Bralant stepped into the breach and offered to spend the evening with Grace.

Violet Bralant* was one of the typists at the Church Army headquarters. She had been there since she was fifteen years of age, when she went to fill a vacancy during the summer holidays and liked it so much that she stayed on. Anyone less like The Doves it would have been difficult to find, and it was surprising that she should in any way have been drawn to them—but she was. Long before Sister Gemmel appeared on the scene, half-horrified, half-amused by their audacious behaviour, she had made an effort, not entirely unsuccessfully, to get to know them. Now that someone had come to take a lead in reaching them, Violet was eager to help. She spent the evening with Grace, and Grace was probably the only member of the gang who did not get drunk that New Year's Eve. Those who did eventually get to Bethany to participate in the party that Doreen had prepared for them had to be almost literally dragged out of the public houses to do so, and when they arrived behaved so badly that the room looked like a shambles when they eventually took their departure.

Ten months after Bethany had been opened, it was closed. The hostel property was to be pulled down and rebuilt, so the little room was no longer available and, it had to be admitted, there was next to nothing to show for its having ever been used as a 'home' for The Doves. They were as abusive and unruly as ever, drunk night after night, and Doreen realized that she could not ask for another chance for them. It seemed as though her work among them had been fruitless, and was now at an end.

But it was just at this point of seeming defeat that it became evident that Bethany must continue. The Doves were filled with indignation—"Here, what have you closed our room for?" they demanded. And when it was pointed out that their behaviour had done nothing to encourage Sister Gemmel to keep it open, their consternation made it clear, not only to her, but to others at Church Army headquarters, that The Doves *wanted* Bethany.

* Miss Bralant was officially appointed to assist Sister Gemmel in Bethany in 1951.

There was, however, no available room, there was no money set aside to rent one, and there seemed ample reason for Sister Gemmel to be drafted back into more apparently productive work.

Then it was that for the second time the journalist in Fleet Street, without realizing it, set the direction for her life. In his office in the London newspaper offices Hugh Redwood, spotlighter of stories of a different character from those usually featured in newspapers, often received sums of money from readers whose hearts had been touched by what they read. The Night Editor had a card index of the people who wrote to him, and of the causes in which he was interested, and one of his correspondents was Sister Doreen Gemmel of the Church Army, who had written to him telling of the change in her life through reading *God in the Slums*.

"Your letter is a wonderful encouragement to me, and I want you to know that I pray regularly for you and your work," he wrote in reply. "This is a great thing that you are doing at Marble Arch . . ."

But no one told him the work had stopped. He had not the least idea when one day he decided to send Sister Gemmel £25 for Bethany from the money that had been entrusted to him that there was no longer a Bethany. He just wrote a typically friendly little letter to enclose with the cheque, tossed it into the tray and turned back into the rush of a newspaper office. But when the letter and cheque reached Sister Gemmel, and she showed them to the Church Army leaders, just at the time when they were wondering whether, after all, something more ought not to be done for The Doves, then it was that the matter was decided. This generous gift, coming out of the blue, must surely be a tangible indication from the God whom Hugh Redwood had met in the slums that Bethany must continue. Nearly twenty years later Sister Gemmel received a letter expressing thanks for Mr. Redwood "because we feel we might not have had a Bethany if it had not been for his cheque".

There was never any question about it after the cheque came. First one room was found, then another, and eventually Bethany was established in the basement of the Church Army headquarters at Marble Arch. It was originally used as the Old Clothes Department, and boasted a private entrance in a narrow mews which was, in fact, the official fire escape. Steep iron steps led down to a heavy door which opened on a bleak, dreary hall with a small windowless storage room in one corner. Leading off the hall was a large room, and beyond that a smaller one. With red brick walls, cement floors, gas and oil meters the basement presented a bleak appearance indeed when Bethany took over, but willing hands turned it into a place which was to become a 'home' to many. The walls of the larger room were distempered and the floor covered with odd bits of lino painted all one colour; and curtains at the windows, pictures on the walls, comfortable chairs, bookcases and a piano transformed it into a comfortable lounge. The smaller room was furnished with kitchen table and chairs, a gas stove, a sink and a dresser while the windowless storage room became 'Sister's office'. And the hall became the storage place for cabin trunks, boxes, suitcases, even cartons containing the only possessions of many a woman who had nowhere to live, and many another who was serving a prison sentence.

How quiet and hidden away it all is, this room in the heart of the world's biggest city. In its hidden-awayness lies one of its greatest strengths, because those who come have been badly hurt in the roadway of life, and when one is hurt one longs so often to hide away.

The motto in this little room is 'Love never faileth'. And the rule? Everyone must have a cup of tea! So they come, this family, from all walks of life, some from lovely homes who have been brought up in great luxury, the wealthy, the not so wealthy, and the very poor, some having had many nights out, maybe on embankment seats. 'Are you going to book a bed or stop out all night?' is an expression often heard in Bethany. Always the greatest power in that little room is the love of God, but always His love brings a challenge with it, and often they say, 'Oh, Sister, let us alone,' and our minds go back to the man possessed by the legion of devils who cried 'Torment me not!'

But as one said who, conscious of failing again and again, sometimes could not face those grey eyes, suddenly stern, that seemed to see right through the flimsy deceptions with which she tried to hide her shame:

"Every time I have gone back to the place, because there it is home—even if you are in disgrace!"

Chapter Ten

LITTLE ANNIE was a character, and she started being one very early in life. A dwarfish little person with deformed feet and a nose that looked as though it had been broken in the boxing ring, she carried to her dying day the evidence of the sins of her father, a drunken good-for-nothing who left his hard-working wife to support their large family of children while he squandered such money as he earned on drink and other women. He hated little Annie, an emotional reaction on which she thrived, glowering at him from under her angrily protruding brows, muttering rebellious and insulting remarks, fighting him with fists and teeth when he beat her. He came into the home drunk one Christmas Day and threw the Christmas dinner of sausage and mash on the fire in front of her eyes, and she never forgot it. Her loyalty to her mother enraged him, and eventually he turned her out of the house. Night after night she slept on the Embankment or on seats in the parks, picking up a meal here, a few pence there, running errands for people or sponging on them. She was well known to some of the officers in Salvation Army Midnight Posts, who were very good to her, in spite of the fact that she had no compunction about upsetting their meetings or shouting rude remarks at them in the street. With her weak little mind she made a useful weapon through which others could fire their cruel missiles. When she found her way to Marble Arch and joined the gang of wild girls there she was like a little wasp to the Church Army, being eminently successful at distracting the attention of audiences at evangelistic meetings. She was incurably curious, ferreting out gossip and passing it on to all and sundry. 'The News of the World' the gang called her, but adding that the *News of the World* only came out once a week while Annie, of course, came out every day.

The first time Sister Gemmel saw her was in the spring of 1937, some months after the opening of Bethany. It was during the time of conference and The Doves were on the steps of the hall one day, waiting for the Sisters to emerge, when Doreen was suddenly aware of a diminutive misshapen figure darting before her and looking up impudently to say, "Are you the Sister Gemmel I've heard about? I'd like to come and see you."

In those days it was an unusual experience for anyone to express a desire to come to Bethany, and eagerly Doreen responded.

"Come and have tea with me tomorrow," she said, naming a time, and sure enough, on the following day Little Annie turned up, discursive, slightly insolent, but on the whole in a good mood. On this occasion she had only one topic of conversation—her friend Mildred. Mildred, it appeared, lived in a room at Drury Lane, and earned her living the easy way. Very pretty, Mildred was, so she had no difficulty in picking up a few pounds whenever she wanted them, most of which she spent on clothes. A great one for clothes, Mildred would throw out perfectly good frocks and hats before they were half worn to make room for new ones. Little Annie had ways and means of disposing of the old clothes for her, besides rendering any number of other services, and what with one thing and another it was doubtful whether Mildred could get on without her. Terrible temper Mildred had, you'd never believe—sometimes she'd just fly at you over nothing. The fights which ensued, it appeared, only served to cement the friendship between the oddly assorted couple, and on this first visit to Bethany Little Annie's attachment to the girl who, free with all men had a friend in none, was evident.

"I want you to meet Mildred," she said, and Doreen's hopes ran high. She thought of the woman of whom the Pharisees said scornfully, "She is a sinner," but to whom her Master said with compassion, " . . . If great sins have been forgiven her, she has also greatly loved." She had never yet met a self-acknowledged harlot, for even the loose-living Ethel was not that. Mildred was one who was beyond the pale indeed, and Doreen longed to reach her.

"I'd love to meet her," she told Little Annie.

"Yes, but she wouldn't love to meet you," retorted Little Annie frankly. "Not her! She'd be furious with me if I took you along. What we'd better do is for me to go along, ordinary-like, and then you come and I'll be surprised like anything to see you, and Mil won't know I knew you were coming . . ."

On the following Saturday, therefore, Sister Gemmel made her way to the house in a side road off Drury Lane where Mildred lived, mounted the rickety stairs to the attic room and stood silently for a minute outside the door, her head bowed, before knocking. The girl who lived within could be antagonized right from the start if she made a mistake—and yet what would be the right thing to do, the right thing to say? She did not know—so she prayed.

How very wonderfully the Lord can use little things! How constantly He used little things Himself as an illustration— a coin, a grain of mustard seed, leaven. When I knocked at the door and Annie showed such great surprise, Mildred was trying on a yellow hat. I was at once struck with her beauty— lovely dark eyes and hair, good features, a beautiful figure—yet marred by that unmistakable mark of 'a lady of the road'.

Without any guile or premeditation Doreen immediately did something which ensured her a welcome. "Oh, my dear, this is the way you should wear it!" she exclaimed, and stepping forward impulsively put both hands on the hat, gave it a little tug, and then stood back. "Look at that!" she said, and Mildred turned to the mirror. The angle of the hat was just right, she agreed smiling, and accepted the grey-clad Sister's presence in the room without question. Little Annie, delighted, breathed a sigh of relief, frowned, and started talking again in the peculiar, grumbling manner to which all who knew her were accustomed.

After that first successful introduction Little Annie became a self-constituted 'contact man' for the Sister of Bethany. Many a publican and his wife were visited by the tall, smiling woman in uniform who came in behind the little dwarfish figure who wanted to introduce 'my Sister'. "You must meet my missus," she would tell Doreen, and took her along to the place where she happened to be working—when she was working. Sometimes 'my missus' was sufficiently intrigued by what her diminutive employee told her about 'my Sister' to pay a visit to Bethany herself. And on one occasion Little Annie, who seemed to know and be known by everyone, said to her:

"Come on, Sister, I'll take you into the Park and introduce you to some of the girls."

Doreen knew whom she meant. 'The girls in the Park' were different from The Doves. Little Annie was proposing to introduce her to the women of the twilight, the women of the world's oldest, most shameful profession, at the very time and place of their hiring. There was something within her which shrank from it—the brazenness, the exposure. But again with that surge of shame came the combating thought that these were the people her Master was seeking, and He must seek them through her.

So she went. Under the shadow of the trees in Hyde Park, after dusk had fallen, she was conscious of encountering a darkness more sinister, more implacable, than the physical darkness of the night. From one little group of women to another Little Annie took her, introducing her to 'Redhead', 'Black Susan', 'Lily— some Lily!' Dimly she saw their white faces, their heavily-blackened eyelids and gash-like lips. They responded pleasantly enough to her friendly greeting and invitation to come and see her at Bethany. Some of them even evinced a superficial interest in her. She was not the sort of person they were accustomed to talking to, and curiosity was temporarily aroused. But the interest was only superficial. All the time there was a strong, invisible pull, like the powerful suction of a whirlpool, drawing their minds away from everything but the business in hand, and one and another would glide away from the group, silently, as the figure of a man strolled by. How remote they were, how difficult to locate, these 'lost women' of London, women of no fixed abode, of whom it is said there are thousands in the metropolis. As she walked along Park Lane later on, returning home, she recalled her friends of years gone by, and how some of them had been presented at Court. Hers had been a very different presentation this night, and she had an indefinable sense of exultation that she

78

should have been introduced, and met on equal terms, these women who were sisters to her for whom her Master, two thousand years before, "must needs pass through Samaria".

If 'the girls in the Park', in spite of several friendly overtures, did not respond to the invitation to visit Bethany, Little Annie never had to be invited—she just came. In the early days she plagued Doreen's life by jumping out at her from alleys and behind pillar boxes, shouting, running alongside, grumbling, arguing, accusing. With the other members of the gang she bashed her way round the first little Bethany room, and when The Doves gradually quietened down Little Annie continued to take the floor on every occasion. She had a way of making a play on people's names, calling Sister Humby Sister Humbug, and a warm-hearted Vicar who was a good friend to Bethany 'Talcum Powder' because he came from a village whose name sounded like that, she said. On one occasion a bishop paid a visit to the basement flat and Little Annie, her hat askew and her face flushed walked straight up to him and said, "I see you've got yer gaiters on!"

"Never backward in coming forward," muttered the others, half amused, half-irritated. But the Bishop asserted that he felt at home in Bethany from that moment!

For all her bad temper and hair-pulling fights with other girls, Little Annie had her religious moods. She made her way up to the penitent form at an evangelistic service on two or three occasions. Then, one day, she came to Sister Gemmel saying that she wanted to be confirmed, so arrangements were made for her to attend classes, and a suitable little grey dress provided for the service. It was somewhat disconcerting to the Sister when, on the very day of the confirmation, a friend of hers on hearing that Annie was in the company exclaimed with amused surprise, "My dear . . . is she being confirmed again?"

"Why?" asked Doreen in consternation. "Has she been confirmed before?"

"At least once!" replied her friend with a twinkle in her eye. It was too late to do anything about it, and Little Annie got through the service without doing or saying anything outrageous.

No doubt previous experience was not without its value, and if, after a day or two of self-conscious quietness she reverted to type and became as gossiping and quarrelsome as ever, there were evidences of reformation in other directions. She began to work for her living instead of cadging it, and if she borrowed money at Bethany, which she frequently did, she always repaid it later.

She had many lovely traits, one of them her generosity. She scrubbed the floor of a flower shop one day so that she could give the money to Bethany, and she so often wanted me to help people. I think it would be true to say that every joy and sorrow of her life has been shared with us. What ups and downs we have had . . . !"

The ups and downs involved subduing her when she was bent on tearing someone's hair out, finding shoes which would fit her little deformed feet, reassuring her when she arrived one night, hair in curlers, certain that she had drunk poison and was on the point of death, and answering the door to her several times a day, for however busy Sister Gemmel was there must always be time for a few minutes' talk with Little Annie. And ere the little waif departed again, satisfied with the glimpse of home, she would say gruffly, "You're not so dusty, well-brushed," and sometimes her hand would reach up to Doreen's cheek, and with a gentler note in her harsh little voice she would add, "I love you!"

The response she got was always the same: "And I love you too, Annie."

Chapter Eleven

WORLD WAR II, after the first few months of what seemed like delayed action, had burst over Britain. More and more people were appearing in uniform, air raid sirens sounded ominously day and night, and everyone was doing something to help the war effort. Even Little Annie got a job as cleaner of telephone wires in a government building, and had to sign a form declaring that she would divulge no official secrets. She called herself a civil servant after that. Christian workers in London went literally underground, and along with others Sister Gemmel spent many hours in the shelters and underground stations into which Londoners flocked at night, talking to individuals and conducting little services. But she did not close Bethany. As often as possible the little room was available for members of 'the family' as she called them, and although they still often arrived drunk, there were times when they were sufficiently quiet to listen to what she had to say. "I never preach a sermon—I can't. All I can do is just to talk to people . . ."

One afternoon she was laying the cloth when the familiar sound of the air raid alarm pierced the air. She had invited Mildred to tea, as on several previous occasions, and the light-hearted little 'lady of the road' had agreed to come. "It'll be an expensive evening for me," she had said with a laugh. "I shan't be able to go into the Park after being with you, so I can't get any money to go back to my room . . ." then, more slowly. "I don't know why it is, I can't go to the Park after I've been in Bethany . . . There's something about this place . . ."

"It isn't something, it's Someone," Doreen had replied. And she prepared for her visitor, as always, hoping that this time Mildred would meet the One whose enabling Hand she herself had groped for in the Glasgow restaurant years before. Christ was the only one who could break the power of that insatiable craving that drove this girl to the life which she well knew would destroy her in the end. But Doreen waited in vain for her visitor that afternoon. Even as she sat listening to the roar of the enemy planes turning back towards the coast, Mildred was lying silent and lifeless in the Park. One of the bombs that rained down during the raid that afternoon fell at Marble Arch, killing some fifty people — Mildred amongst them. In the very place where she had so often stood after twilight, death suddenly overtook her.

Little Annie was the first to discover what had happened, and came to Bethany with the news, weeping bitterly. Some hours later Sister Gemmel, called for to identify her in the mortuary, stood looking down at the limp figure of the young woman she had come to love. This 'unfortunate' had not yet been weary of breath, but death had cut her life short all the same. The musical voice, the quick, fierce temper, the equally quick flashes of affection, all the little characteristics that went to make up the Mildred so few really knew—silenced, quiet now.

> *Take her up tenderly,*
> *Lift her with care,*
> *Fashioned so slenderly,*
> *Young, and so fair . . .*

Had she, even in that last moment, grasped the outstretched Hand, Doreen wondered. Had she gone, recklessly, blindly over the precipice, or had she, unknown to any other, 'mercy sought and mercy found'? There was no answer to her question, and she knew she could not penetrate the veil beyond which Mildred's soul had slipped. She only knew that had the girl, even in that last moment, sought mercy, she had found it.

This sudden death of one of their number had a very sobering effect on the other members of the Bethany family, and it was a strangely assorted group of women who stood by the little prostitute's grave as her coffin (which they had paid for) was lowered into the ground. And Doreen found they listened a shade more quietly when she spoke solemnly of life beyond the grave. One evening she was sitting at the piano in Bethany, with a group of the girls around her, singing a hymn about meeting loved ones in Heaven, and suddenly she broke down and wept.

"Sister, what's the matter?" they demanded with consternation, and said to each other, "She's tired . . ." "She's doing too much . . ." "It's the heat . . ." "She needs a rest . . ." But she looked at them, her eyes brimming with tears, and said vehemently:

"I'm not tired. I don't need a rest. It's not because it's hot. It's because I don't know how many of you I really will see again in Heaven. I don't know how many of you really do trust the Lord Jesus, and He is the only way . . ."

They became silent, slightly embarrassed at this glimpse into a depth of feeling they had not realized existed. Then Grace, with a flash of unusual insight, said slowly, "If *you* care like that, how much more *He* must care . . ."

It was while the war was still at its height that Sister Gemmel paid her first visit to Holloway Prison. She was to go there innumerable times in the years ahead when, as an official visitor, she had access to the cells and could go to sit alone with the women inside. On this first occasion, however, she had been asked by the resident Church Army Sister to speak at a Bible Class one Sunday afternoon, and as she walked across the paved courtyard of the great, castle-like building which lies right alongside the wide London street with its stream of cars and buses passing by, she tried to imagine the feelings of the many women who were inside those thick, grey walls.

As I stood in front of those tremendous prison gates, almost frightening in their strength and austerity, as well they should be, I was glad there was a tree at one side. I looked up through it to the sky above and thanked God for His message of salvation. I knew that if God could change a proud and self-satisfied heart like mine, He could certainly change anyone within those grim prison walls. Is there any degree of sin in God's sight? I believe, as one writer has put it that 'the ground is level at the Cross'.

May not many have to re-think their evaluation of religion if this is really so? Is it true to say that one who is a regular church-goer, living a perfectly respectable and law-abiding life, is in the same need as a man or woman who has done a crime deserving an eight- or nine-year sentence? Is it really true that one may have one's name on the electoral roll of a church, or on the location roll of a prison, and there is no difference in God's sight? Is it true that if Hitler repented in his last moments I kneel at the Cross with him? I believe it is, or I have no message for any man or woman, in or out of prison. Is this revolutionary thinking? But then, I have proved that the message of the living Christ is completely revolutionary, and turns a life upside down. How significant it is that after the parable of the two sons (when the one said he would go to work and did not, and the one who said he would not go, did) that the Lord said these words, "Verily I say unto you, that the publicans and the harlots go into the Kingdom before you." And He was talking to the chief priests and elders, the people who constantly said, "Lord, Lord."

In response to her knock a little door opened in one of the big gates, and she stepped inside the wide prison entrance, with its rooms for the keepers of the gate on one side, and the room where visitors had to wait on the other. She was conducted past the wide entrance into which the police cars and the Black Marias swept over the cobbled stones, through to the large, rather bleak church building.

Here were gathered a group of very ordinary-looking women, dressed in blue print dresses and some wearing navy blue cloaks. I think what struck me most of all was the singing of the hymns—lovely singing in those bleak surroundings. It brought a lump to my throat. Why? Because of the pathos of it all, the power of sin in lives, the loneliness that sin can bring—and I think because I knew that 'but for the grace of God' I could have been wearing that dress . . .

When the time came for her to speak she rose to her feet and started in her usual chatty manner to talk about a word that was constantly being heard in those days—MISSING. She told of someone she had heard speaking on that very word recently and how, for a second or two that seemed like many minutes, she became silent, as though her mind had gone a blank.

"Why? Because only a few days before to her home had come that dreaded War Office telegram to say that a beloved brother had been reported 'missing'.

"Recently I went to a garden party where I had to speak, and I noticed that the Vicar's wife was busily caring for everyone's needs, completely forgetting herself. Yet one of those present told me during the afternoon, 'She has just had a telegram to say her boy is missing.' Oh! That awful word—MISSING.

"Up in Scotland once I saw a shepherd who seemed to know all his sheep individually. He knew the greedy ones, the shy ones, the wayward ones, the silly ones. And he knew, when nobody else did, when one was missing, and he knew which one it was, and until it was found he couldn't rest . . . He'd leave the flock in charge of a sheepdog, and go off with his shepherd's crook, stopping every now and then with his head cocked, listening, listening, hoping to hear the bleating of the sheep that was lost, so that he could go and find it . . . That's what the shepherd is like. He *must* find the ones that are missing, and he listens, listens, hoping to hear their cry, so that he can go and find them.

"Does the Shepherd hear *your* cry . . .?"

She went many times after that, and later became an official prison visitor, which gave her the opportunity for personal talks with women alone in their cells—the work she loved the best. Her initial visits were not always encouraging, and one of the staunchest existing members of the Bethany family described her first reaction to the entry of the tall, grey-clad figure into her cell.

"I was almost at the end of my sentence—no prospects, no thought of what I was going to do, didn't even care—no hope of life ever being any different . . . Then one night my door opened and in walked Sister Gemmel. She said she'd been asked to help me. My reactions to that were not very complimentary. Another curious person, I thought (don't want no truck with her!) and I asked her how much she wanted to know—and don't preach religion to me! I told her to hide behind her cloak of religion, and if she wanted to pray to get on with it! Her reply to that was, "I will—and I will help you." She is still helping me, after years, in a way that is unbelievable to anyone but the one who has experienced it. She found me a job when I was released—clothed me—I still wasn't interested in why she did it, other than just curious. On first arriving at Bethany I said, 'Get me away from this place as quick as you can', but where I would be today without Bethany I don't know. I have failed many times, but what God has done through her is just past all understanding. Just let me tell some of the happenings of the 'Love Never Faileth'. I have never stayed very long in a job. On one occasion I had walked out and intended to get right away again into the blue. I was no good at this religion, it was not for me. I had been a big drag on Sister Gemmel, and couldn't face those eyes that spoke of Jesus. I got another job, then something inside me said, 'Write and let her know'. I did, and told her I would be changing trains at Victoria. When I got off the train and walked to the barrier, there she was waiting for me. My heart stood still. After all I had done, she was there—I still mattered! Could I run away? No, I was being held by the everlasting arms.

"I wouldn't do it again—so I thought. I lasted about six weeks—walked out of another job. No sense of responsibility, no thought of anyone but myself. Yet every time I have gone back to the place I wanted so badly to get away from at first, a peace comes over me, and I feel secure." (So many of them say that—*it's the only place where I feel secure.*)

Don't for one minute think she condones—far from it. I have sometimes been unable to bear the look, and believe me, the words of reproach are worse to me than a two-edged sword. But deep down you know in your heart it is because she cares, and understands just what is needed to bring you nearer to the Lord ... And all this has not been in vain. I still fail, but also know that I can go to Him and ask for forgiveness and be cleansed, even though I have been the chief of sinners. He loves me and wants me ... I matter to Him. I've proved it, and why? Because He sent Sister Gemmel to Holloway Prison to teach me of Him ..."

One of the greatest joys of the Bethany workers was to entertain a woman who had just completed her prison sentence. When prisoners were to be discharged at eight o'clock in the morning, either Sister or Violet Bralant would go inside the prison gates to meet them, and walk down the wide stone path to the busy thoroughfare of the Pentonville Road, and join the queue waiting for a bus.

Does that sound a small thing? Will you picture coming out alone to a world perhaps greatly changed since you first went into those prison gates? Would you be glad to be met by a friend who wanted only the best for you and was willing, yes, and hoping, to be your friend for life, entering into all your joys and sorrows? How greatly blessed we are in having this lovely Bethany room to bring our folk to! They come out of prison at eight o'clock in the morning, so we come straight to Bethany for breakfast—eggs and bacon, tea in a dainty cup again, made in a teapot and as many cups as you like!

Chapter Twelve

ONE SUMMER afternoon in 1950 Sister Gemmel was sitting in her little windowless office opening on to the hall with its inevitable pile of boxes, cartons and suitcases, waiting for the members of a Mothers' Union to arrive. A party had been arranged for them in Bethany, and she was occupying her time by looking through her correspondence, There were letters relating to the annual holiday in Tankerton to which she took members of her rowdy, convention-defying family, and she smiled as she remembered the reaction of the C.A. chief of staff when she first announced her intention of embarking on this experiment. "You will pray for us, won't you?" she had asked, and with significant emphasis he had replied, "My dear—it'll be *you* I shall pray for!"

Next she turned her attention to the circular letter which she had just had printed to send round to the increasing number of people who wanted to help the Bethany work. "It's prayer we need most," she told them, and looked through the list of the women for whom she was feeling specially burdened. Careful always to avoid disclosing names she wrote of them by initials only.

Thank God for 'B'. Used to be drunk every night for many years. Four years ago quietly in a church, while on holiday, gave her life to Christ.

Please pray for 'S'. Her boy of eighteen took his life a year ago. Is groping her way back to God.

'Y'. Has had education and profession, lost nearly everything through drink.

'E'. Also had education and profession in the world. Has served many prison sentences, now beginning to make good progress, has asked for prayer.

'V'. Journalist and reporter, no work, money or home, said the Cross was all emotion, but admits a Presence in Bethany and is beginning to believe there is such a thing as new life in Christ. 'H'. For thirty years has taken drugs, now believe she has claimed God's strength to overcome, but has still not got His peace.

Suddenly the telephone rang. Lifting the receiver she heard, "Sister, will you take this call?" and then she was put through to someone who said in a cultured voice:

"I'm phoning from the —— Club. There's a lady drunk in the lounge. Will you come and take her away? Take a taxi, don't spare any expense! We don't know what to do with her!"

Sister Gemmel had no time to explain that she was waiting for thirty members of a Mothers' Union to arrive, nor did that worry her. As she often said afterwards, when telling the story, "Anyone can deal with thirty Mothers' Union members!" And when, some time later, she had ushered Veronica, dead drunk, into their midst, she told them that they were seeing 'Bethany in action!' She did not realize that she herself was being introduced into an area of human need which hitherto she had not touched. She had been mildly surprised at being asked to help with a woman who was the worse for drink in a smart London club, for until this time her experience had been mainly among those who lounged around public houses not usually frequented by those in the higher strata of society. She wondered whether the woman would rebuff her friendship when it was offered, and prayed that she might make the right approach. When the taxi drew up in front of the imposing entrance to the Club she was welcomed with relief by the Club secretary, who was waiting on the steps, and on entering the door found herself confronted with a woman who was talking as wildly as The Doves when in their cups. Acting on the conviction that 'the Colonel's lady and Judy O'Grady are sisters under the skin' she walked up to the drunken woman with a smile, spoke to her soothingly, and started piloting her to the door. When they were both in the taxi and bowling along towards Bethany, the woman turned to her, glassy-eyed and thick-voiced, and said, "Do you know, I am the only British woman to hold the —— Diploma?"

Veronica was, indeed, a gifted and highly-qualified professional woman whose career had been ruined by drink. She was an alcoholic, and like all alcoholics, when the craving for drink took her, she was unable to resist. At first the bouts were short-lived, but as they became longer and more frequent she found herself travelling the path into solitude familiar to so many. There was the dawning realization that the careless desire for drink was becoming an insatiable craving; that there were times when she *must* have it, whatever her duties might be; then there came the discovery of it by others; removal to another district; money problems, interviews with the bank manager; the bottles smuggled into her rooms, then stacked away empty in the cupboards, behind the wardrobe, anywhere; the landlords who refused to go on letting their rooms to her; the removal to another district, a poorer one; the sense of shame; above all the fear of being without that for which the whole being craves. The fear of being given notice to quit, the fear of loneliness, nothing was so bad as the fear of being without a drink when the craving came. "I'm afraid—*afraid I'll have to do without it!*"

When, later that evening, Veronica was sobered up sufficiently for Sister Gemmel to take her back to the rooms she was renting, it was only to find that the landlady refused to admit her.

She had evidently been very difficult. So at midnight we were back at Bethany, she and I. I managed to get her a bed in a hostel for that night. The following day it was possible to arrange for her to go to a home for alcoholics in the country.

Veronica's gratitude for what Sister Gemmel considered 'so small a service' was touchingly sincere, and although she failed again and again she always found the door of Bethany open to her and she thankfully took advantage of it. She seemed to find relief in sitting at the piano with her fingers darting over the keys, for she was a talented pianist. Sometimes the telephone would ring and it would be Veronica wanting to talk to the one person who, although grieved, never seemed shocked or horrified at her. On one occasion she had been invited to Bethany for lunch, but got no further than one of the great London railway termini, where the police soon saw that she was drunk, and with typical sympathetic tolerance elicited from her the name and address of a friend. So it came about that a call was put through to Bethany.

"Are you expecting Miss —— to lunch?" Sister Gemmel heard as she held the receiver to her ear. "She's on No. 15 platform here, drunk. Will you come and fetch her?"

For the second time I set out to fetch Veronica home, but this time with no fear of my reception. She had managed to say on the phone, 'I only want to come to Bethany.' When I arrived at the railway police station I was met by a tall inspector. I looked up at him and said, 'I think you've got a friend of mine here?' Slowly a smile spread over his face and he said, 'Yes, I think we have a friend of yours here!' I count it one of the greatest privileges of my life to have such friends and know a little how my Lord must have loved the name of '*friend* of publicans and sinners'. Not helper or benefactor, but *friend*, with all that that means. The four men who broke up the roof to get their friend to Jesus had to be willing to give themselves, their time, yes, and their money! They would have to put that roof back or pay someone else to do it. So too must we be willing to give if we would be a friend to those we seek to win.

Once again Veronica was brought back to Bethany, and it was hours before she was sober enough to get on her way again. Some time later she moved up to London, into a room not far from Marble Arch, and one evening Sister Gemmel, going to visit her there, was met at the front door by the landlady.

"The police have been here today," she was told, "she's been taken up the worse for drink. If you want to find her, you'd better go to the police station." To the police station she went, only to find that the police had let Veronica go. For hours that night Doreen stayed in the basement flat in the mews with the light shining at the top of the iron stairs, hoping that the woman, drunk though she was, would find her way there. But it was not until the following morning that news was received of Veronica.

The telephone bell rang, and a man's voice at the other end of the line explained that she had spent the night in the police station—would Sister Gemmel come along and fetch her?

Veronica was bowed, her head low with shame. When she saw the familar, grey-clad figure come towards her she said, almost despairingly:

"Can I come back to Bethany again—would you let me come even after this?"

"Can you come back to Bethany!" exclaimed Doreen. "Can you come back? My dear—of course you can! I've come to fetch you home."

In the years to come many others were to stumble, almost dumb with shame, down the iron steps that led to the basement flat, having been charged in court with being picked up drunk the night before. Many a time was Doreen to look compassionately into the anguished eyes of women whose last memory before awaking to find themselves in a cell in a police station was sitting in a public house, or walking into a café for a cup of black coffee hoping they could pull themselves together sufficiently to return to their bed-sitting room quietly enough not to arouse the suspicions of the landlady. As time went on Alcoholics Anonymous, and hospital almoners heard about the Sister at Marble Arch whose long patience and faith in God was proving effective in the lives of some whose case seemed hopeless, and often sent to her women whom they felt she could help. But Veronica was the first of that long, sad stream of enslaved women known as 'alcoholics' to come to Bethany, and there were times when it was a fight for Doreen to keep on believing that this woman who declared that Biblical proof of a life after death was 'not tangible enough' for her would one day put her trust in a Saviour whom she could not see.

A year after that first telephone call she was able to go and live with one in whom she found real love, and a home. But there were still ups and downs. How she is linked with telephone calls! One day her voice in great distress came, 'I need you desperately. I want your help!' Alas, we know in Bethany how very real are those S.O.S.s. Although she now lived a little distance out of London I was with her in just over an hour. Fortunately she had left the key in the door. When I went into her room I thought at first that she was dead. She lay across the bed completely unconscious and ashen grey. Do any disbelieve in the reality of Satan? That afternoon I fought with him as he laughed at me and said what a fool I was to think that she would ever be different. I told him he was a liar and that I knew she was going to know Jesus as her Saviour. All that day I stayed with her till Gillian came home from work, then returned after eleven at night. All through the hours we waited for her to regain consciousness. At last she stirred and awoke dazedly. Could one ever hear a sadder prayer than hers after she had asked us to pray for her? 'Lord, don't let this change her love for me!' Does He not know the utter loneliness that craves for clean, pure love, a *safe* love? And, too, craves for those to whom love can be given, those who will receive it. How Jesus must have treasured the love that stooped to wash His feet with her tears and dry them with her hair!

Two years after she had first been brought to Bethany Veronica was taken ill, and weakened as she was by the years of drinking, she lacked the physical resources to combat disease, and it was evident she was not going to recover.

The night before her passing we stayed beside her bed quietly singing the hymns she had come to love. No thought of 'not tangible enough' was in her mind now. "I think I saw God," she whispered quietly once, after coming out of what had seemed like unconsciousness. "He said, 'Don't be afraid. I'll look after you and her'."

It was three weeks after Veronica had died that Doreen, on her fifty-eighth birthday, opened an envelope which contained a number of torn scraps of paper and a letter. She recognized the scraps—they were little text cards she had given to Veronica, who had torn them up one night when drunk. Mystified, she turned them over in her hand, then opened the letter and read:

93

"I am getting Gillian to write this and making her promise you will have it on your birthday in case I have finished my weary journeying by then. If I haven't—well, maybe I shall give it to you myself. I want you to know you have been my 'bestest ever' friend, even more to me than my own mother and father. There has never been anyone like you. I wanted so much to bring you down to my level, but you have tugged me up to yours. I shall be at the Gates waiting for you. I know this now, and I believe it. It's been hard to understand, but like my music I have at last 'got it'—and for keeps. Those cards I tore up when I was tight, they are to be the symbol to you that all the old things are torn out of me, and all the new ones are in . . ."

Doreen bowed her head, tears in her eyes, but they were not tears of sorrow. She felt the same as she had felt the day, a few months before, when she stood alone in the little mortuary in which lay the lifeless body of 'the wee lamb', Ethel, with whom she had walked around the streets so many times in the old days. Big, defiant, drunken Ethel, whom she vividly remembered rolling along beside her one night, bursting every now and then into loud singing—singing not of a ribald song, but of the hymn,

> Oh, come let us go and find them
> In the paths of death they roam,
> At the close of the day 'twill be sweet to say
> I have brought some lost one home.

Ethel, too, would be 'waiting at the Gates' for her, she knew that, for in her case, also, long patience and faith had been rewarded. Alone in the mortuary that day, with memories surging in to quicken her emotions, she had knelt down and with tears streaming down her face had softly sung:

> At the close of the day 'twill be sweet to say
> I have brought some lost one home.

Chapter Thirteen

"OFFICER, WILL you come and evict two people from my flat? They won't go—they're just sitting here and refuse to move. Please come at once and put them out."

The request came over the phone to a police station in an agitated feminine voice, and in a short time a young constable was marching round to the address he had been given. It was a well-furnished flat in west London, and on entering it the policeman was somewhat surprised to find only three people in it—an angry woman obviously under the influence of drink, and a tall Church Army Sister in uniform and her assistant who smiled pleasantly at him as he entered. Not unnaturally he hesitated a moment, uncertain as to which one was to be evicted, but he was not left long in doubt.

"Which was the lady who telephoned to the police station?" he asked.

"I did. Turn these women out of my house!" replied the angry woman imperiously. "I will not have them here!"

The arm of the law, however, had taken in the situation. The bottles of champagne, the smell of alcohol, the woman's incoherent manner all told their own story. He glanced quickly at the Sister in her grey uniform, then addressed the owner of the flat again.

"How did they get in here?" he enquired. "Did they force their way in, or did you invite them to come, Madam?"

"I invited them to come," was the answer. "And they had the impertinence to try and stop me getting at my own drink, and when I told them to get out they refused to go. Turn them out!"

"Well, madam, I'm afraid I can't do that," said the constable in a patient tone of voice. "You see, you invited them here. They're not molesting you or stealing your property. I'm afraid

I haven't the authority to turn them out." Whereupon the angry woman walked determinedly, if somewhat unsteadily, to the phone, dialled the police station number and demanded that someone be sent round immediately from the police station to evict the policeman who had come and refused to do what she told him.

"All part of the day's work of Bethany," said Sister Gemmel with a laugh as she recounted the story later. "We never know what will happen, and there are times when the women who come to us for help treat us as though we were their worst enemies!" She suffered physically at their hands on occasion, and an injury received from being knocked down by a woman in a violent temper caused constantly recurring disability for years. And in the early days of the Bethany work a parcel was delivered at her door containing refuse so vile that, unwrapping the paper in which it was concealed, her senses of sight and smell were so powerfully assailed that she reeled back, nauseated. Too loathsome to be thrown in the dustbin, the filthy bundle was eventually dumped, on a bombed site to which she stole with it after dark. Mingled with the sense of shame was an almost exultant joy as she remembered that her Master had been spat upon, had borne 'shame and scoffing rude', and this was an opportunity to share, in her little measure, that experience.

For the most part, however, the ever-growing Bethany family tried her love and patience without intending to do so, and the humorous side of some of the situations in which she found herself was never lost on her.

What times we had with Ursula, for instance! Divorced from her husband, who had been given custody of the two children, Ursula had been in and out of practically every mental hospital in London. One evening I took her to Waterloo to go and stay with a friend of Bethany who is always ready, when able, to have one of our family for a visit. I saw her into the train . . . imagine my surprise when, about a quarter of an hour after I got back to Marble Arch (by underground!), Ursula, having left the train at Clapham Junction appeared in a taxi. To add insult to injury, the taxi-driver came in demanding from us 15s. 6d. to cover the fare and cost of drugs which he had stopped to buy for her on the journey. There were other taxi incidents with her—one when a taxi-driver opened the door holding Ursula's passport in lieu of fare! Another day the taxi meter registered 12s. 6d. waiting outside the National Assistance Board to which she had been driven to get money.

A sense of humour was one of the factors which helped to keep the Sister's sensitive spirit from being overwhelmed by the misery and shame of the women she loved.

Bethany was well in action now. By 1951 it had become evident that Sister Gemmel could scarcely carry on unaided, and Violet Bralant had her heart's desire fulfilled when she was released from secretarial work to give her full time to Bethany. Full time it certainly was, for the iron gate at the top of the steps that led down to the basement flat was unpadlocked at 9.30 a.m. and rarely locked again until 11 p.m. or even later. As the calls increased, the work could not have been maintained without the loyal, uncomplaining, cheerful presence of 'The Coolie' as Gladys Aylward* affectionately dubbed her. To Sister Gemmel herself the relief and strength of this comradeship was incalculable.

How good it was to come back from visiting, or police court, or prison to find the gate of Bethany open, instead of padlocked during her absence, and to see Miss Bralant giving someone a cup of tea in the kitchen! We never know who will be behind that door—it may be an alcoholic, a drug addict, someone straight from prison—or a Bishop! How many quiet chats have gone on between Miss Bralant and one of the family in that little kitchen, chats which have meant so much to desperately lonely souls almost at the end of their tether. And how careful

* Gladys Aylward, the well-known missionary, had at that time returned from China and was living in a mews near Marble Arch. She was a frequent visitor to Bethany, and the family knew and loved her well before her return to the East in 1953. She still writes and sends presents to her 'Bethany friends'.

she has been to see that every small need (so great to the one in need) for a night at the hostel has been met, such as towel, soap, face flannel, comb.

Among the many requests for help that came to Bethany was one which resulted in a story demonstrating the many paths along which love will travel to seek and find one who is lost. It started, as far as Sister Gemmel was concerned, one morning in 1952 when she was going through her mail and opened a letter from which a rather old photograph fell out. As soon as she saw the notepaper she knew it was from Hugh Redwood. It was written from his newspaper office, and she started reading the letter eagerly, for she knew the busy editor would not write without a purpose. The letter commenced in the manner he adopted towards the Salvation Army slum post captains to whom he had long been an elder brother, and she felt honoured to be in the same category.

"Dear Little Sister,
When I was speaking in Southampton just over a week ago, I made some reference to you and to Bethany .

Three or four days later I had a very moving letter from a Mrs. Baker whose daughter Naomi has been missing for a year, and is believed to be frequenting the neighbourhood of Oxford Street. She said she had been told that once a girl had taken up this kind of life there was absolutely no hope for her and she begged me to say whether I shared that belief, and if not whether there was any chance of contacting and rescuing her daughter.

Naturally I told her I did not share the belief, and I asked her if she could let me have a recent photograph of the girl so that I might show it you on the off-chance that you might know her or somebody else who did.

The enclosed photograph has come this morning . . . Is it possible that she is known either to you personally or to any of your flock? And even if not, will you put her on your prayer list, as I am doing, in the hope that somehow or other we may establish contact for her own sake and her mother's?

Naomi Baker . . . ? She had never heard the name before, and the rather indistinct, six-year-old photo of a young woman who appeared to have no distinguishing feature resembled no one who came to Bethany. When she asked one or another of the women who made their way down the iron staircase to visit her if they had heard the name they shook their heads, and said, "No—never seen her!" when shown the photograph. But the name was put on Bethany's private prayer list, and as it was mentioned regularly in the quietness of God's presence, it became mentally imprinted on the memories of the two workers at Bethany.

They did not only pray, however. Armed with that indistinct photo one or another of them would set off down the Bayswater Road, or along Piccadilly, or round the narrow streets of cosmopolitan Soho, looking for a woman who might be Naomi Baker. They searched in vain at that time, but although they eventually ceased their deliberate searching, they continued listening for the woman's name, and more than two years after receiving Hugh Redwood's letter, Sister Gemmel heard it at last.

She was sitting in her little office one day talking to a woman, mother of four illegitimate children, who had come to see her. The woman was concerned about a suitcase, and in the course of her rather incoherent story Sister Gemmel interjected the question:

"But whose suitcase is it?"

"Oh, not mine. It's Naomi Baker's suitcase . . ."

"Naomi Baker! Naomi Baker!" Sister nearly jumped with excitement. "We've been looking for her for months. Where is she?"

"She was at the Institution, same as me," was the reply, "Don't know where she is now . . ."

As soon as her visitor had gone Doreen picked up the telephone receiver and got in touch with the welfare worker at the north London institution. Yes, Naomi Baker had been there, but some time ago had been sent to the Church Army hostel in Bryanston Street at Marble Arch.

"Why—that's right on our very doorstep!" exclaimed Sister.

She was up the iron stairs the next minute, and hurrying along the street to the hostel.

"Has a woman called Naomi Baker been coming here at nights?" she panted. The hostel, like all of its kind, only provided accommodation for the night, not for the day, and those who slept in the beds in the dormitories or cubicles left in the morning after an early breakfast.

"Naomi Baker? Yes. There was a woman of that name here for a few nights, but we haven't seen her for some weeks. No . . . haven't a clue where she is now. You know how it is with them. They just go out saying they'll be back in the evening, and then we may never see them again."

Doreen knew. The trail was lost again almost before it had been found. Nevertheless, the Bethany workers were encouraged rather than otherwise. They knew that Naomi Baker was alive, and that she was in London. These facts had been brought to their knowledge they believed as direct evidence that God was working in answer to the prayers of many people. Their hope was quickened, even though many more months passed in silence. Then, one evening, Sister Gemmel, having been away all day, phoned Bethany and heard the voice of her assistant, usually so deliberate and slow-speaking, say excitedly:

"Naomi Baker is found! She's in the Mile End hospital. She's just had a baby."

It was too late to go that night, but as early as was reasonable to expect admittance to a ward Doreen was at the hospital, at once eager and apprehensive. That a mother's prayers to find her lost child were answered filled her with joy. It was the sense of the responsibility that was hers, as the messenger of that mother, which made her apprehensive. If there was that about her or her words which repelled, there might be a hardening rather than a softening on the part of the daughter. Very earnestly she prayed that she might make the right approach. What sort of woman would Naomi prove to be? Excitable? Resentful? Confiding? Secretive? Was she still involved with evil companions, or was she alone in her helplessness and need? Doreen knew the sensitive shrinking of the soul wounded and diseased through the continual searing of the conscience, and that clumsy handling could do irreparable damage. One glance at the woman lying in the bed two places from the window answered some of her questions. The eyes that looked dully out from the dark, heavy-featured face, were unexpectant, without interest. There was no excitement here, no anger, no feeling of any sort, it seemed. Doreen felt she was looking into the eyes of one whose soul had died in a body that continued reluctantly to live. The locker beside her bed was empty, with none of the personal possessions such as were on the lockers of the other women in the ward—bottles of orangeade, tins of talcum powder, combs, vases of flowers. The nightdress she was wearing was supplied by the hospital. She was destitute, and alone.

Gently Sister Gemmel introduced herself, sat down by the bed, and told Naomi of her parents' constant prayer that she might be found and of their longing for her. "And others have been praying for you—all sorts of people in different parts of the country have been praying for you . . ." As she spoke the listless eyes focused on her face began to betray an awakening surprise and interest, and when the question was put, "Would you like to see your parents?" the woman, after a moment's hesitation, said slowly, "Yes—if they really want me . . ."

With what joy I telephoned to Mr. Redwood, and how great was his excitement when he heard the news! He immediately wrote to her ageing parents and gave them the wonderful news —but sad news, too, as Naomi had had her fifth baby, this time a little coloured one. We arranged for them to come to our Mother and Baby Home in Paddington, and although it was the time of the Railway Strike her parents managed to make the journey to London, and what a reunion that was! The Sister there said it was one of the most touching scenes she had witnessed.

Joys such as the finding of Naomi and seeing her restored to her parents were offset by the tragedies of such as Catherine. The only daughter of titled parents, she had started drinking recklessly at an early age, and by the time she first came to Bethany, a woman of over forty, she was an alcoholic, had served many prison sentences, and more often than not when she found her way down the iron staircase leading from the narrow mews, she was penniless and homeless. She had become inured to 'sleeping rough' and all the efforts of her family to ensure that at least she always had a decent lodging at night were unavailing. An allowance which could only be drawn by daily application to a bank, and therefore not squandered at once, was spent not on the food and lodging for which it was intended, but nearly all went on drink. Catherine's mother, with whom Sister Gemmel got in contact, admitted that she was always rather relieved now when she heard her daughter was in prison. "When I lie in bed and hear the rain beating down, I know that at least she's got a roof over her head . . ."

The workers at Bethany loved Catherine. She was not quarrelsome or noisy or demanding of attention, and in her soft, cultured voice always expressed gratitude for help received. Nevertheless, there were times when, sitting with her in Bethany's quietness and security they felt they were talking to one on the very brink of the precipice beyond which realms of darkness were waiting to engulf her. The easing warmth of the room with its message 'Love never faileth' and its promise of power for a new life comforted the woman temporarily, but she had yielded weakly to the craving for drink so long that she had no desire for anything else now. The darkness claimed her in the end. She finished serving a prison sentence shortly before Christmas one year, and she was met at the gates and carried back to Bethany for a tasty breakfast, then provided with a new outfit bought with money her mother had sent for her. Arrangements had been made for her to have a Christmas holiday in a home in south England, and she went off there. But the craving for drink was stronger than self-respect or gratitude. She made her way back to the old haunts in London, and one morning, early in the New Year was found, an empty handbag beside her, on a seat in the Embankment Gardens, She had died of exposure.

This was one of the saddest happenings in Bethany's history, and never shall I forget my visit to prison when I had to tell the news. Everyone in that place who knew her loved Catherine, I think, and women and officers alike were sad at what they heard. I well remember the sorrow of one of the women (also a member of our family), and how we wept together in her cell that night.

Perhaps the secret of Bethany's power to attract those who would have nothing to do with organized Christianity lay in those three words, 'we wept together'. It was not only the assurance of a welcome and a chat over a cup of tea that drew women whose lives were dominated by their own vice to that basement flat at Marble Arch. There were many doors inside which they could be assured of a welcome and a chat—the fellowship of the pub is too often more real than the fellowship of the church. Nor did they come only for the practical help which they undoubtedly received when their needs were made known, though receive help they did. A great deal of the Bethany workers' time was taken up with visits and phone calls and letters to various public bodies and private people able and willing to assist the destitute, the ex-prisoner, the down-and-out. But there were other organizations to which application could have been made with equal effect. The magnetism of Bethany was the love which could laugh with delight over another's good fortune, which went on trusting when confidence had been betrayed again and again, which bore no grudges, above all, the love that wept.

"It was when I saw the hurt in her eyes that I *knew*" said one who thought she had got beyond feeling. "I saw what I was doing to *her* . . ." If she herself did not care any more how low she sank, whether she lived or died, it gradually dawned on her that Sister Gemmel did. It was the love that exposed itself to being hurt that was the magnet at Bethany.

"I wouldn't change those four walls at Bethany for any palace. I've worked for ladies of title and lived in their luxurious homes, but that basement flat in the heart of London, has far more riches than all their beautiful homes—it holds love, peace, security, understanding for souls who don't understand themselves. It is holy ground. Jesus is there. It is the only home I have—I matter —I have a friend who knows all about me and loves me just the same. I have turned my back on Jesus many times, but have found Him waiting for me at Bethany, seeming to say, 'I knew you would come "home" because I sent you here'."

Chapter Fourteen

JOYCE PEDALLED slowly along the road that led through the quiet residential district to her home, oblivious of the beauty of the trees and shrubs that were just beginning to open out into fresh life after the barrenness of the months of winter. Her mind was occupied with what she had been hearing at the church mid-week meeting she had attended, and with the speaker, a tall, grey-haired Sister in the uniform of the Church Army, who worked in a place called Bethany at Marble Arch. She had spoken of the delivering power of God's love in the lives of people commonly known as 'down-and-outs', confirmed drunkards amongst them, and Joyce, deeply aware that her human love had failed completely to deliver her own husband from the slavery of alcoholism, had been gripped.

It was nearly eighteen years now since, as the young wife of a service-man billeted overseas, it had dawned on her that Ronald was drinking too much. Normal social life involved drinking for both of them, but when she realized his increasing dependence on it she decided to give it up, hoping thereby to help him to break it off. It made no difference. He continued drinking, not only in the company of others, but as time went on, at home, often in secret. "The hair of the dog that bit you!" Joyce knew the significance of that phrase, and could picture how Ronald, with a hangover in the morning from heavy drinking the night before had been cajoled into tossing down a glass of whisky before starting on the duties of the day. "Come on, old chap, just one and you'll feel fine again! The hair of the dog that bit you, you know!" And sure enough just one drink did seem to clear his head, and give renewed self-confidence. But the fatal cycle of craving had started with it, and as it gathered momentum body as well as mind was affected. He commenced having those strange convulsions which startled her so much at first, and then dismayed her when she knew what they were. She usually contrived to keep him in bed until the bouts were over. That was the one thing for which she never failed to be thankful—he was always amenable when drunk, and would do what she suggested without argument. Had it not been for that it would not have been possible to keep the fact of his enslavement a secret, not only from friends and neighbours, but even from the family. Only the doctor knew. She smiled wryly as she remembered how, longing for someone with whom to share this burden, she had confided once in his brother, who had flatly and indignantly refused to believe her. After that she knew that she must carry the secret alone, and wondered how much longer she would be able to hide this thing of which he, as well as she, was so ashamed; how much longer the explanations, "Daddy is tired and rather irritable; leave him on his own"—"Daddy has to go to hospital; the doctor says he'll only have to be there for a few days," would leave the children slightly anxious but unquestioning.

She slowed to a standstill as she arrived at the opened gate of her home, and slipping off her bicycle wheeled it into the garage and entered the house. Low-ceilinged, with oak beams, lattice windows and little nooks and crannies, and with a garden sloping down and melting into the soft shadows of a wood, it was a home in which her personality could express itself perfectly, and she loved it. This evening, however, she entered mechanically, her mind still absorbed, and as she moved about in the tastefully furnished little dining-room, laying the table for the next meal, she found herself longing to talk personally to that tall Sister who seemed so certain that the living Christ could save even alcoholics. She herself was fast getting to the place where hope could hold no longer. All the medical treatment Ronald had received had failed to effect a lasting cure. She glanced at him, tense with apprehension, as he entered the room. She always seemed tense now, even when he had come out of a bout and she knew there would be a period in which things would be more or less normal. But she must not let him know how she was feeling. She made a casual remark and smiled brightly at him trying with words to drive back the silent fears which she dared not express. Fear of

106

what the alcohol would eventually do to him; fear that he would make mistakes at work which would lose him his job; fear that he was running into debt; fear that the neighbours would find out; fear that the children would find out. Fear, too, that he would sense that she was losing confidence in him.

The compassion she felt for him was inexpressible, welling up, unable to find an outlet, until it seemed that her heart must burst. For she knew what lay behind it all. She knew how, in the early days, a drink or two had somehow fortified him, overcoming that shrinking sense of inadequacy which no one but she so much as suspected was there. She knew how the responsibility of his position in those days of the war had preyed on his mind, and how when things went wrong and lives were lost he wondered if he were to blame, going over and over again the decisions he had made, the orders he had given, lest some fault lay with him. Always it was a few drinks that served to dull those acute sensibilities, not her comforting and reasonable reassurances. And when at last he began to realize what she already knew, that the drink was now his master, she had seen the grim-faced struggles to resist, and the shame after each failure. She knew how he fought to keep a grip on himself and keep his job, not for his own sake but for the sake of her and the children.

"It's because I've let you down, isn't it?" he had said sadly when she told him one day, rather awkwardly, that she had come to Christ, and found that she had a surprising inward satisfaction now. "It's because I've let you down . . ." The self-reproach of those words smote her heart. Her fervent avowals that this new experience was something quite apart from him failed to convince him, although he said no more about it. That was ten years ago, and she knew that she could never have got through them, never have shielded him from exposure, had it not been for the comfort and strengthening that had come through the minutes spent silently on her knees before God, and the remarkable answers she had received to her earnest, sometimes almost desperate prayers.

But the strain was beginning to tell on her, and as she saw the bouts occurring with increasing frequency, noted Ronald's lack of zest for anything but the bottle ("Life isn't worth living without a drink"), discouragement was fast changing to despair over him. Her faith for herself was unshaken. She knew the promise of Christ to all who trust in Him was true, "I will never leave thee nor forsake thee." But strive as she would for steady faith that Ronald would be delivered, it fluctuated and flickered like a guttering candle. Perhaps that was why the memory of the Church Army sister remained, for she obviously believed that no matter how deep in sin a man or a woman had sunk, Christ *could* save. Joyce longed to ask her if she really believed there was hope for one who was so gripped by alcoholism as Ronald, but her natural reticence prevented her until, as spring passed into summer and things were going from bad to worse, almost in desperation she wrote to Sister Gemmel one day, briefly outlining her position, and asking for advice. The reply came, suggesting a visit to Bethany.

And so, early in August she went, found the narrow little mews, descended the iron stairs and stood in the dark porch at the foot waiting for the door to open. It opened outwards, rather to her surprise, and she stepped back quickly to avoid being knocked. A laughing voice apologized for the awkwardness of the entry, urged her to come inside, and she was conveyed across the dark hall with its stacked-up suitcases, trunks, boxes, into the spacious square-shaped room with its comfortable chairs, its bookcases, its vases of flowers, its pictures and its one text—'Love never faileth'.

Years later, remembering that first visit, Joyce wrote:

"The first thing that struck me on going to Bethany was that it was just like the early Church, something I had never come across before, not having been brought up in a Christian home. In this parish I had never seen anything like it. I had thought it wasn't for Christians nowadays. Then to go to Bethany where it's as natural as breathing to pray and everything centres around the Lord—well, it brought home to me in full force what I was missing. And oh, the sense of hope and security the moment you go there! Burdens just seem to disappear."

During the following months Joyce not only went several times
108

to Bethany herself, but persuaded Ronald to go, too. He was willing to do anything to obtain freedom from this slavery even acknowledge his helplessness. "The new life in Christ is the only permanent release to the alcoholic," Sister Gemmel told him, and he tried to believe, and to live this new life. "It won't work," he said to Joyce hopelessly. "It's not for alcoholics."

Everyone else thought so too, apparently. "Of course, God *CAN* do anything," said some who professed and even manifested real faith in Him in their own lives, "but he doesn't work in that way nowadays". And when a Christian psychiatrist told her it just was not possible for an alcoholic, while drinking, to have an experience of God, the cloud of depression and despair that overshadowed her was so thick, so heavy, she felt she could not bear it. Her nerves were taut, and her mind burdened by her fears to the extent that she could not think for more than a few moments at a time of anything else now. That interview with one from whom she had hoped for a strengthening, reassuring confidence nearly shattered her. If Ronald had really got to a place where even God could not reach him (there was never a day when he was not drinking now) what hope was there? She felt she could not bear this alone any longer. Blindly, scarcely knowing what she was doing, she ran to Bethany.

Although she had been there before and talked frankly about her problem, it had always been with restraint, and in an objective manner. She did not readily reveal her feelings. But this time she could not control them, and in the seclusion of Sister Gemmel's little office, where so many women had sobbed out their stories, she poured out all that was burdening her heart.

The bottles, hidden all over the house . . . The fear of people finding out . . . The men who, knowing the doctor had forbidden Ronald to drink, nevertheless urged him jovially, "Just one . . . come on, now, just one!" . . . the pathetic fights to hold out . . . the need now for sleeping tablets . . . the failure of all the treatments . . . the hopelessness . . . even the Christian psychiatrist had said an alcoholic couldn't have an experience of God while he was in drink . . . There was a relief in confiding it all to someone she knew would understand, but when she came to this last blow, this apparently conclusive verdict, she became almost incoherent. She had tried to believe that God would deliver Ronald in answer to her prayers, but if it was impossible for Ronald to have an experience of God now . . .

The clear, expressive voice of Sister Gemmel broke gently in on her grief.

"But, my dear, *who* says it is impossible? Did Jesus say it was impossible? Jesus said that with God all things are possible . . ."

Joyce's attention was arrested.

"I am so sorry, my dear, you feel it is all so hopeless. I promise you it isn't, though I know it's hard for you to realize it at the moment. You are *right* in what you believe. As I told your husband, the new life in Christ Jesus is the only permanent release to the alcoholic. You and I both believe that. We know it's true, so we must hold on for him. After all, when the four men brought their friend to Jesus and let him down through the roof, it was their faith the Lord marvelled at—we do not read that the man himself had any faith."

You and I believe . . . we must hold on for him . . . Back in her home, these words repeated themselves over and over in her mind. *You and I . . . we . . .* Emotionally exhausted, she realized that she was nevertheless eased, and hope was beginning to rise slowly again. She was not in it alone any more.

It was the turning point for her, and all fear of a nervous breakdown dissolved from that time. Her faith was renewed. "Now I knew someone who really believed all things are possible to God—with no 'buts'." But something else had happened. For the first time there was someone really sharing the burden with her, someone eagerly awaiting news of any development, whether good or bad, someone to whom she could write or telephone or go at any time—"the joy of hearing her voice and encouragement when I phoned!" (How great a part the telephone was always playing in Bethany!) Above all, there was someone else who was praying. At times when she found herself unable to compose her mind sufficiently to pray, when she found herself slipping down into the doubt that led to despair, she would reassure herself as she reminded God, almost urgently, that

Sister was praying. She clung to Sister's rock-like faith when her own seemed to be failing, and through the months that followed she needed it. Ronald's condition was deteriorating rapidly until by the following spring they both realized that he was on the verge of D.T.s again.

They were critical days. Ronald, trying desperately to pull out of the bout, and failing helplessly, spoke several times of suicide. He was getting worse and worse, in bed now, terribly restless, craving for sleeping drugs to give him oblivion. Joyce phoned Bethany daily. 'With God all things are possible,' was the message that came again and again, and just when things looked most hopeless it proved to be true.

Ronald was tossing in bed, craving for a drink, drugs, anything to assuage this terrible, consuming desire, yet still struggling feebly to resist, and Joyce was there with him. "Remember that in Christ is all our hope," Sister Gemmel had said to her, and with the knowledge of the faith and prayer of those at Bethany fortifying her against yielding to the apparent hopelessness of the situation, she spoke of Him. "There is a way out, through Jesus Christ our Lord," she said. "There *is* a way out . . ." She knew so little about what is known as 'personal dealing', and seemed to have none of the key 'salvation texts' at her finger tips. But she did know that Jesus is alive, and that He can rescue from the strongest bonds of craving. The room was charged with unseen forces that night, and the words that came from Joyce's lips came unbidden, unpremeditated, as though she were inspired. Perhaps she was. As she talked, even the consciousness of the Sister at Bethany, on her knees in prayer, faded, and she was aware of another Presence, One before whose power doubt and fear dissolved, and she spoke with increasing conviction.

"There *is* a way out—through Jesus Christ . . ." And then she looked at Ronald and said, "Shall we ask Him to do it—shall we pray . . . ?" He nodded, and closed his eyes, and the miracle happened. In the quietness of the bedroom this man, in the condition in which it had been asserted it was impossible for anyone to have an experience of God, listened as his wife prayed and at the end just said, solemnly and emphatically, "Amen".

111

That was all. He uttered no other word. Then he opened his eyes and glanced at her, leaned back on the pillows again and murmured,

"Oh, what peace . . . I can sleep now." He turned over on his side, closed his eyes again and Joyce, as in a dream, saw his body relaxing and that he was falling asleep. Then she looked at the table by the bed and saw the sleeping tablets—untouched.

She could not know that night what lay in the future. She could not see him then as he was to be in the months and years ahead, interested again in wholesome, normal things, with a zest for work, an enthusiasm for gardening, a delight in watching the birds come as he scattered crumbs for them, an enjoyment in music. She could not see him refusing with smiling steadiness those cajoling invitations to have, "Just one, old fellow—one won't do you any harm." The conversation together in which he was to tell her his impressions of her "after she turned religious" had yet to be held as the days unfolded, with the thrill of laughing together over it, looking at each other without any barrier of unspoken fears yet to be experienced. That night, sitting in the bedroom watching him breathing deeply and regularly, fast asleep, scarcely able to believe what had happened, she saw only him, and those sleeping tablets by the bed—untouched.

Chapter Fifteen

THE LORRY came screeching to a standstill as the driver, cursing, jammed on the brakes. In the pool of light cast by the headlights stood a tall, graceful girl who had jumped from the cab of the lorry ahead of him and run out into the road.

"What the blazes are you up to?" he shouted. "Tryin' to kill yourself or something? What d'you think you're up to?" The girl came round to the side of the lorry.

"I want a lift to London," she said, her face rather white.

"Well, that chap's going there," said the lorry driver irritably. "Why didn't you stay with him?"

"He frightened me," the girl replied simply. The lorry driver understood, and said, "Asked for it I reckon . . ." then, more gently, "You're too young to be out by yourself this time o' night, thumbing lifts to London. If you belonged to me I'd spank you and send you home."

The girl laughed. Her courage was returning.

"They wouldn't have me there," she said, "my mother told me I'd better get out, so I got out. I want to go to London. Will you give me a lift?"

The man hesitated a moment, then shrugged his shoulders and leaning over, opened the door. "All right," he said. "Jump in. No affair of mine what you've been up to." The girl heaved herself up into the seat beside him. "What part of London are you going to? Marble Arch any good?"

"That'll do," the girl replied, settling down beside him. She deposited a zip-fastened bag on the seat and smiled. "Marble Arch, anywhere you like. It's all the same to me."

The man glanced at her and grunted. She was devoid of make-up, still in her teens, her skin was fair and clear, her eyes bright. Nevertheless, there was a boldness, a recklessness about her attitude that he recognized, and he answered briefly:

"Yep. I guess it's all the same to you."

Ruby's eyes were fixed on the bright beam of light that raced along the bends and turns of the Great West Road, lighting up houses, hedges, trees, and flinging them into the darkness again as the lorry sped on towards London. She was burning her bridges now, with a vengeance, and an underlying fear was crushed by the excitement she felt as she plunged into the unknown, loosed completely from both the restraint and the security of home. "You'd better get out altogether, Ruby," her mother had said in a voice that was dull with despair as the girl, indifferent to the atmosphere of tension in the home, prepared to go out again that evening. "We can't go on like this—you out night after night, coming back at all hours. We can't stand much more of it, your dad and me. We done what we could, we done our best. We got the child . . . You'd better get out altogether."

"O.K." Ruby had said calmly, ignoring the sense of shock that suddenly seemed to freeze something deep within her. "O.K. I'll get out altogether. Better take a thing or two . . ." Upstairs, where her two-year-old daughter lay asleep, she had picked up a few clothes, rammed them into a bag, and came downstairs again. The Salvation Army *Songsters' Hymnbook* lay on the table where her father had put it when he came in from choir practice. The hearth-rug looked flattened and dirty, though it would be clean and fresh again tomorrow after it had been shaken outside the back door. The old clock ticked away amongst the muddle of letters, coins, keys, that always littered the mantelpiece by the end of the day. It was all so familiar. It was home. And now she had been told to go.

"So long," she had said, looking defiantly at the weary, strained faces of her parents. Then she had gone out, slamming the front door behind her.

Sitting now in the lorry, refusing to heed that sense of shock within, she turned her thoughts towards London. She had had a couple of drinks in a public house, just enough to give her a pleasurable sense of excitement and assurance, before thumbing a lift, and the effect had not yet worn off, in spite of the fright she had got on the previous lorry. As they came to the suburbs, and

114

the empty, lighted streets that led up to the West End, however, slowing down only when the traffic signals shone red, she knew that soon she would be alone, and wondered what she would do. It was two o'clock in the morning as the lorry bore up the Bayswater Road to Marble Arch, and came to a standstill in Edgware Road.

"Here you are," said the driver. Ruby sprang down to the pavement, and looking up at him before slamming the door said:

"Bye, bye. Thanks very much for the lift."

"Take care of yourself," he replied, as he slipped in the clutch and prepared to move on. "S'pose you think you can do that all right."

Ruby stood on the edge of the pavement and looked down the long, deserted street, where the glare from some of the lighted shop windows cast grey shadows across the pavements. All sense of belonging anywhere had gone now, as even the lorry hove out of sight. No one knew where she was, no one would know what she did. "No one cares, neither," she thought, flinging the reproachful thought at her parents, although she knew it was not true. But a feeling of utter abandon possessed her, half-despairing, half-pleasurable. She was homeless. There was nothing to hold her now, no place here that tugged at her heart, always drawing her back because she belonged there. She was alone in London, and she had eightpence halfpenny in her handbag, and it did not matter what happened.

A man appeared from one of the side streets, and strolled in her direction. She took a quick breath, then looked him straight in the eyes, boldly . . .

When, sometime later, she found an all-night café and went in for a cup of coffee and egg and bacon, she had a £1 note in her bag, along with the eightpence halfpenny.

So she launched out on a life which carried her up and down on an exciting, dangerous current. Restless, eager, daring, she was never in one place long. Sometimes, when 'business was good' she lived in hotels, spending the money her clients gave her freely. At other times, the money that had come so easily all gone, and 'business' slack, she placed her suitcases in railway station cloak-rooms, and went off to 'sleep rough', lying on seats in the parks, or stretching out on the rubble of bombed houses. Every now and then her restlessness drove her from London, and buying a penny platform ticket at one of the great termini she would board a train to some port or provincial town, there to pursue the same old life in different surroundings. But she always came back to the metropolis, and her familiar haunt on Half Moon Street. "Back again, Ruby?" the policemen would say affably as they saw her standing there. They took her in charge once in a while, and she spent the night in a police cell, paying her £2 fine next day at the magistrates' court along with others of her ilk, but she bore them no grudge on that account. They knew that she was independent, not the member of a gang or vice ring as some of the girls were, peddling drugs or trading in sex perversion, although her visits to some of the gloomy night-clubs in Soho acquainted her with what was going on. They saw her standing blatantly at the corners of streets, her ancient profession evident to all, in spite of the fact that she wore no make-up—'war-paint' her father had called it. They had her sized up all right, they thought—just a common prostitute, nothing less and nothing more. They would have been mildly surprised had they known what was in the suitcases that she carted from one place of temporary abode to another, for incomprehensibly, this girl of the streets collected and hoarded, not clothes or garish jewellery, but books. Most of the women she met in her familiar haunts were too restless and shallow in mind to do any reading beyond what they could flit through in picture papers and women's magazines and cheap novels, but Ruby found little satisfaction in any of these. There were depths within her soul that cried out to be fathomed, and there was something about poetry that probed those secret regions as nothing else did. The rapture of the soaring skylark, the gentle influences of melancholy, the unutterable loneliness of the sea breaking on the grey stones, all plumbed that invisible being imprisoned within the daring, audacious Ruby, so that tears came to her eyes and she would sit in some squalid room in a tenement house absolutely oblivious of her surroundings. And as the words

116

vibrated like chords in her mind, a yearning was awakened for something deeper than the somewhat mournful satisfaction afforded by the poetry itself.

She knew what it was she was yearning for. That was the amazing thing. Years later, to a girl on the brink of the same life that she had lived, she wrote, "Over the years I felt the hand of God stretched out to me, but I paid no heed, although I knew that I wanted Him, wanted Him desperately." Not without effect had been the uncompromising, constant emphasis on the facts of God and of a Saviour to whom sinners could come, which she had heard repeatedly as a child in Sunday School or Gospel meeting. She knew what she needed, and yet, in the words which she read again and again, in Francis Thompson's 'The Hound of Heaven':

> *I fled Him, down the nights and down the days;*
> *I fled Him, down the arches of the years;*
> *I fled Him, down the labyrinthine ways*
>   *Of my own mind; and in the mist of tears*
> *I hid from Him, and under running laughter.*
>   *Up vistaed hopes I sped;*
>   *And shot, precipitated,*
> *Adown Titanic glooms of chasmed fears,*
> *From those strong Feet that followed, followed after.*

It was not until she met Peter that the pursuing Footsteps caught up with her at last. Peter was some twenty years older than she, and he had been an inveterate drunkard and gambler until, as he explained, Jesus Christ had saved him. When he came to Jesus, he said, the old cravings were taken away, and he was free of them. "He can do it for you, too, Ruby. Come along with me to the meeting tonight," he urged her when he met her from time to time, and she yielded easily enough to the persuasion, partly drawn by respect for the only clean-living man who would be seen with her, and partly by the old familiar atmosphere of a Salvation Army hall. And there it was that one evening, at the close of a typical Salvationist meeting with its hearty singing and its brass band and its simple earnest preacher pleading:

117

a tall, young woman, head held high though tears were trickling down her cheeks, walked to the penitent form at the front and knelt down there. The Hound of Heaven had overtaken her.

What Peter had told her proved true, and her life was changed. She got a job as an office cleaner and her evenings were spent at the Salvation Army hall, or with the Salvationists in their open-air meetings, where she readily told what had happened to her.

"What could wash away *my* stain?" she asked in the words of a favourite hymn. "Nothing, nothing but the Blood of Jesus." For months this continued, and she got in touch with her parents again. Then she went home to see them, and her own little daughter to whom, from time to time, even in her wild life, she had sent toys and gifts.

And it was while she was there with them, in the circumstances most likely to hold her firm, that she encountered temptation that took her unawares.

Perhaps she was too sure of herself. Perhaps she thought she was strong now, and could play with fire without being burned. Whatever the cause, the outcome was that meeting a young man whom she had known as a child, she agreed to spend an evening with him. Alas—the way was too easy, the path too well trod, and almost before she knew it, she fell again that night. Her spirit was clouded after that, and when she returned to London Peter noticed that something was wrong.

"You're different," he said. "You're not right with God. What is it?" Irritably she denied it, but as the weeks passed, and she knew what was to be the consequence of that fatal evening of recklessness, discouragement at herself gave way to despair. Ashamed now to go to the hall where she had become one of the most prominent 'trophies of grace', the casual, easy-going conviviality of the public houses seemed the only refuge for her, and by the time her child was born she had drifted back where she was before.

When she had her first baby, at the age of sixteen, she was

conscious, young as she was, of passing abruptly from childhood to womanhood. From that time on, however wild and irresponsible she might seem, underneath the outward carefree show was the knowledge that she was not a child, not even a girl, but a woman. With the perception of maturity she looked at the hard, painted faces of the older women who lived as she did, saw in their eyes the death of the soul, and knew that one day she would get like that. The realization had often chilled her, and she had tried to ignore it, but she could not. She was a woman and she knew, just as she knew other things of which a child is ignorant.

But if with the birth of that first child she passed into womanhood, with the birth of this child she passed in a new way into motherhood. Never in her short passionate life had she loved anyone as she loved this little boy. She spent her only happy hours with him, she tended him, fed him, bathed him with an absorbing, unselfconscious devotion. Whatever means she might employ to provide a living for them both mattered little. What mattered was that Paul should be clean and comfortable, warm and happy, have good food, good clothes, toys to his heart's content—and that she could spend as much time with him as possible. For two years he was the centre of her existence, the one for whom she lived. And when he was two years old, trotting about, a chubby, sunny-tempered little boy, her love for him was faced with a bitter choice, for as she looked at him, she saw the dawning of an unusual intelligence, the reaching out of a little mind that could recognize both good and evil, she knew that her life was no life for him. And that if she wanted the best for him, she must let him go. He must be adopted, and she must part with him—for ever.

> *Measure thy life by loss instead of gain,*
> *Not by the wine drunk, but by the wine poured forth,*
> *For love's strength lieth in love's sacrifice . . .*

Love's strength in Ruby was tested in those days. She made her choice, saw him adopted, and returned to the room that had been home when he was in it to lie on the bed, her body shaken with sobs that seemed to come from the very depths of her being.

She clenched her fists and pressed her knuckles against her forehead in an agony of longing, and paced the room as one in a torment when she pictured him, his little brows puckered and eyes bewildered, calling, "Mummy! Mummy!" After six weeks of it she went to say she must have him back, she could not live without him; and was told, kindly but conclusively that it could not be. The child was legally adopted, she had signed the papers, and she no longer had any right to him.

With a compassion that stemmed from godliness the couple who had adopted the child let her see him, but after one meeting she knew the emotional strain for her son as well as for her would do harm, not good. She must stay away, and if he did not see her he would soon forget her altogether. Perhaps that knowledge was the bitterest pain of all, and for his sake she bore it, although time and time again, if she saw a little fair-haired boy in the street her heart seemed to stop beating as she thought it was he.

Then she heard that the couple who were his parents now were emigrating to Australia. So that was the end. She would never see him again. He had gone out of her life for ever, and because the grief was so great she hardened herself to forget in the way that was easiest and most familiar. And, all unaware of the Hand that was outstretched still, she drifted back to the place where she had alighted from the lorry, at two o'clock in the morning, eight years before. She became known as one of the wildest, most reckless women who walked after dark along the Edgware Road where it empties into Marble Arch—within three minutes' walk of Bethany.

And there it was that the following Footsteps from which she had fled overtook her again. The sisters of the Church Army, 'fishing' passers-by in the streets to persuade them to attend the meeting in the little chapel in the mews, saw Ruby, and one of them, greatly daring, approached. Again and again in the following weeks the Sister invited the tall, bold-looking girl into the meeting, and after the girl had several times accepted the invitations, suggested she should come with her to Bethany. And so it was to Bethany that Ruby came.

The first thing that attracted her when she got inside the little kitchen was the dresser. So surprising it was to see anything so homely as a dresser, with its cups hanging on hooks, and plates and saucers standing up behind them. She did not remember when she had seen such before anywhere in London—certainly not in the hotel rooms, or the dingy 'bed-sitters' to which she was accustomed. And next to the dresser was a gas stove with a kettle boiling, ready for a cup of tea. It made an indelible impression on her mind. It was like home—and there was always someone there, someone who was glad to see her, anxious about her, ready to plead with her and even to speak sternly to her, but with a grief which somehow made it difficult to answer back.

Slowly the hardness and bitterness was eased out of Ruby's soul, although for months there was little enough to encourage those who mentioned her name day by day, as they bowed in prayer. Only she knew the deep, deep thoughts of her own heart, the returning sense of shame to take the place of brazen impudence; only she knew the wordless prayers, the weak, pathetic little reachings out for forgiveness 'when none but God' was near. And only she knew the cries for mercy when, realizing that another little life was coming, she felt she could never go through again the parting she had endured from Paul.

And only the One Who saw the tears and heard the cries knows how there came across her path a labouring man, nearly twice her age, with a simple faith in God. Only He knows how that meek labouring man, knowing what she was, should nevertheless love her with a reverence and respect that no one else ever showed her, and take her as his lawful, wedded wife. "My husband—he treats me like a queen and makes me feel like one." And only He sees her in those moments when now, even as a happy mother of children, satisfied with her family life, she still is conscious of a deeper hunger than even "the best bliss that earth imparts" can satisfy.

"If any man thirst, let him come unto Me, and drink." She has her own peculiar way of coming. She puts her elbows on the kitchen table in her little home in one of the great cities of the country, and draws her mind away from the distractions of her household, constantly added to by the neighbours' children who

121

come freely in where they are always sure of a welcome, and projects it to the place where she is always sure of a welcome. She thinks of Bethany; she starts at the dresser, with its green cups and saucers, and the bread bin with the sliding lid. She thinks of the gas stove, and the kitchen table with the oil-cloth covering, and the brown teapot. Then she passes through the door into the larger room, with the piano, and the bookcases, and the carpet on the floor, and the simple, comfortable chairs. Lastly, she remembers the pictures on the wall—the Good Shepherd, the Vigil, Christ in Gethsemane, and the text 'Love Never Faileth'. Then she goes still farther, seeking the One to Whom Bethany is her way. Quietly she repeats the words, "Draw nigh to God, and He will draw nigh to you." And then, in the quietness of her own soul, she becomes aware that He is there, and that His Hand is outstretched still . . .

Chapter Sixteen

A WAGTAIL was picking its way delicately across the smooth lawn that ran down to the edge of the lake, and Sister Gemmel, sitting with a companion on the garden seat outside the long, low, half-timbered house, watched it with delight. She had come for a week-end to this quiet place set amongst meadows and woods, with the Sussex downs in the background, where even bird life seemed different from that of busy London with its roaring traffic and heavy atmosphere, and she breathed in the fresh, fragrant air appreciatively. Nevertheless her mind went back, again and again, as though drawn by a magnet, to the twenty-six years she had spent in Bethany, and as the hours passed—and she sat out in the soft sunshine, her pen sped rapidly over the writing pad on her lap, reviewing the past.

What warfare, what peace, what storms, what calm! And I think the greatest feeling of all is *joy*. How joyous is the Lord's service when we are where He means us to be. Surely Nehemiah was right when he said, 'The joy of the Lord is your strength!' Love and joy have been so intermingled in Bethany. I have known and experienced for so long that only 'love never faileth'. We can work till we have two or three nervous breakdowns, we can talk till we have no breath left, and it will be all of no avail because only love never fails. Love heals every wound and breaks every barrier. How well I remember the morning when I sat in my little office with one who thought I had failed her and let her down so badly because I had had to give her 'friend' up to the police (the only time I have ever had to do this), because this said 'friend' was indeed dragging her down to within a yard of hell. She refused to say a word to me, so we sat for about ten minutes, and all the time God was saying to me, 'My love can heal every wound and break every barrier.'

I can hear it today as clearly as I heard it in that little office years ago, and it is as true today as it was then, and ever will be.

Sometimes people have said to me, "Don't you get depressed in your work?" *Depressed*—how could we get depressed when we see always what we believe our family will become in Christ? And if we didn't see that how could we carry on? As Oswald Chambers so rightly says, 'depression is of the devil'—however the depression may come, through overwork, tiredness or ill-health. No, depression is never of God. Heart-brokenness, yes, that must surely come our way. If we know nothing of the suffering, can we ever fully enter into the *fellowship* of the suffering?

And how does the suffering come to Bethany? So often through a telephone call. We pick up the receiver to hear the voice of an almoner, an employer, a friend, even the police, saying, 'So-and-so is drunk.' And perhaps they had been doing so well, overcoming temptation, winning battles (and how often we remind ourselves that we see the failures but not the times they have overcome), and now, down again in the depths. And we look into our own hearts and wonder have we failed them through lack of prayer, lack of fellowship? Be that as it may they must not stay down. We must go where they are and by love and friendship bring them back. I am reminded of the story of a man standing under a lamp, looking worn and dejected. Another came up and said, 'Can I help you? 'Yes,' was the reply, 'if you're willing to come down to hell with me.'

Doreen leaned back in her soft garden chair, her pen idle as memory took her back to days and nights in that room underground near Marble Arch, where she had spent hours on end trying to quieten one distraught woman after another, half-crazed with drink or dulled by drugs, sometimes near to suicide. She remembered the two smartly-dressed girls who had been brought to Bethany one Sunday evening, and who she learned, after they had come several times, were members of a drug-running gang. Every night, from twelve until five in the morning, they were in clubs, quietly obtaining the drugs which it was their job to take to clients in various cafés. She thought of the one, Susan, who had been drawn again and again to Bethany by some power she knew not what, and who had said time and time again, "I'll have to stop coming here. I can't go on leading this double life." "Don't give us up, give up the other life," Sister had replied.

One Saturday morning she came to Bethany, and I said to her, 'Susan, if we can get you right away now, would you be willing to come?' She said she would. I phoned the Carliles (Bill Carlile, the old Chief's grandson, was head of the Church Army at that time), and they said, 'Bring her down here.' So I took her to Edenbridge, where they lived, and she stayed there about six weeks. She behaved very wildly at times—sitting on the stairs in her nightie, saying she was going out; having no drugs made her morose, abnormal. Eventually I had to go down to be with her, and slept on a camp bed in her room, never leaving her.

Then, one midnight, she started packing two suitcases, saying that she was going, 'All right,' I said, 'if you are determined to go, you can go. But I'm coming with you.' 'I don't want you,' she replied. 'I'm coming all the same.' She had threatened to go before, but this time she really went, leaving the house carrying two suitcases. She had to go along a country road, and I followed, but realizing I'd need a torch to see the way went back into the house. I caught her up as we were approaching a bridge over a stream, and Susan sat down, tired, on her suitcases. Then suddenly she got up, said she was going to throw herself into the stream, and ran towards it.

The moon had come out by this time, and Doreen, running after her and catching her by the lapels of her coat, had seen the wild expression on the fair, thin, pretty face. Had she been alone that night the waters would have claimed her. As the wiry little figure had writhed to be free, Doreen had stood, praying aloud, and eventually Susan had quietened down, returned to her suitcases, picked them up and again started walking up the hill. Then she had stopped again, and put down the suitcases.

I heard dogs barking—we must have been near to kennels. But Susan was quieter, and after we had talked a little she lay down on the ground, put her head on one of the suitcases, and went to sleep. I sat down on the other suitcase, watching her, praying, but conscious of a deep, unaccountable peace. After about twenty minutes Susan awoke, quite normal. She had kicked off her shoes somewhere, but she walked quietly back to the house with me without them. I got her to bed, then went back for the suitcases!

She had been 'within a yard of hell' that night, and it had been no easy matter eventually to get Susan installed in a children's home, where she became a reliable member of the staff. But a year after Susan had first been put on the list for prayer, that went to those friends of Bethany who prayed for those they never saw, Sister Gemmel wrote, "To God be the glory for the change in this life—and to the one in charge of that home who truly has had Christ's own patience with her."

One of our greatest blessings in Bethany has been our prayer partners. How often I have said this to those innumerable people who come into our lovely Bethany room and at once are conscious of the 'atmosphere' as they call it. I can then tell them that over three hundred people all over the world pray for this little sub-basement flat at Marble Arch. It is *steeped* in prayer. Is it any wonder that even atheists sense the peace here? Three or four times a year a letter is sent to these wonderful prayer partners of ours, giving names specially to pray for. Only the other day I told a woman in her prison cell, "Over three hundred people all over the world will be praying for you." A look of awed amazement came into her eyes. So many of our family have no one to pray for them—can you wonder at this look coming into their eyes when they hear that over three hundred people are going to pray for them?

I am often asked how we got our name, and I love telling people how that came about. At our headquarters we use abbreviations, and when Bethany first began I was given a folder with the initials R.G.W. on it. This puzzled me, and when I asked its meaning, I was told it stood for 'Rough Girls' Work'. 'Do you really think I am going to have it called that?' I asked. I was really roused, and went to one of our Church Army Deaconesses, who had been a tower of strength. She was completely of the same mind, and said, 'Sister dear, we must call it Bethany.' How grateful I was, and ever have been, for that heaven-sent inspiration. It would be quite impossible for me ever to thank God enough for the very great privilege that has been mine in being a member of the Church Army family— the caring, the love, the interest, the trust they have given me. I sometimes picture in my mind the day when I shall 'know even as I am known', and in that day I shall thank my Lord for Hugh Redwood, 'my adjutant', and Wilson Carlile. The first for his pen, the second for showing me Jesus, and the third for giving me such a wonderful opportunity of service. It may be that someone reading this is at the crossroads of life, even as I was. God may have put this book into your hands that you, too, may be called to this joyous (and suffering), way of answering His call.

In the years of my pilgrimage I have learned, I hope, much that God has meant me to learn. But oh, how much has gone unlearnt because I was too lazy or too busy or too deaf to hear. How true it is that 'by receiving we learn'. One of the things very deeply laid on my heart is the great longing of our Lord that we should 'all be one'. How deeply we must grieve Him by divisions —and surely divisions can only come from the enemy? There can be no division in spirit amongst those who truly love and serve Him and who are born of the Spirit; with those Satan has no power to divide, by whatever label they may be known, or by whatever device Satan may devise.

Another thing I have learnt, that has been borne in upon me as much as all else, is the complete barrier that criticism and judgment erect between the respectable and the outcast (for lack of a better expression). Until we, as Christians, come to the place where we cease to take the world's standard of sin as our standard, and realize afresh that *the ground is level at the cross*, that barrier will remain. We are so apt to think that some sins loom higher than others in God's sight, and that such things as pride, jealousy and bad temper will not have such severe judgment. Do we find this in Christ's teaching? Was it not the 'good', religious Pharisee who was publicly rebuked in St. Luke, vii. 36-50? Had he ever been subjected to the temptation which had assailed this woman who, in her great love, washed the Master's feet with her tears? Did he know the loneliness of of an outcast's life? No, he would have been surrounded by friends, by those who looked up to him, his life would have been lived in comparative comfort, perhaps even luxury. No prying, shocked condemnatory looks would have been cast on this leader of religion. And yet he was rebuked.

God give us the grace and humility to come down from our self-made pedestals and, kneeling first at Thy feet, to go out to where are those *we* call outcasts and tell them of the love of Christ who came to where we were that He might lift us and them to new ways of living—to *His* way of living. "I am come that they might have life, and that they might have it more abundantly."

LOVE NEVER FAILETH